MW01173493

The Undeniable Truth

By Meekeeyah R. Lee

Definitions:

Undeniable – Plainly true

Truth – The body of real things, events and facts

Season – A period of the year associated with a particular activity, event, or holiday

Scripture:

John 8:32

And You will know the Truth, and the Truth shall make You free.

Ecclesiastes 3:1-8

To Everything there is a season, and a time to every purpose under the heaven:

A time to be born, and a time to die; a time to plant, and a time to pluck up that which is planted;

A time to kill, and a time to heal; a time to break down, and a time to build up;

A time to weep, and a time to laugh; a time to mourn, and a time to dance;

A time to cast away stones, and a time to gather stones together; a time to embrace, and a time to refrain from embracing;

A time to get, and a time to lose; a time to keep, and a time to cast away;

A time to rend, and a time to sew; a time to keep silence, and a time to speak;

A time to love, and a time to hate; a time of war, and a time of peace.

Dedication

To My Children. Your Mom is so much more than you ever thought. And so are each of you. I love all of you.

Introduction

The Undeniable Truth of this book is that the events that you will read are truth and facts. Plainly. This book is about my life as a Spirit Filled Child of God, before coming to know this. This book is going to show you what a person goes through Spiritually as well as physically. The Bible states in Isaiah 46:10 That God declares the End from the Beginning. The Bible also says in Jeremiah 29:11 I know the thoughts that I think towards you. Thoughts of peace, not of evil, to give you an expected end. God is a God who is Intentional. The definition of intent is the state of mind with which an act is done. Another definition says: what one intends to do or bring about. So, in considering what these scriptures are saying and the definitions we see that in order for God to get the glory from His creation He orders things and situations to happen to bring about the end that He intends. Is this a bad thing? Not at all as you will realize at the end of this book. The Truth, plainly and undeniable.

Season 1

What Happens Before You are Born

Deuteronomy 30:19 I call heaven and earth to record this day against you, that I have set before you, life and death, blessing and cursing: therefore choose life, that both you and your seed may live.

Generational curses are real. How they come about is by people not choosing to follow and obey God. People have made deals with the evil one just for some instant pleasure. Not caring or knowing that the end result would be to a later generations harm. What you are about to read in this section will show you both sides. Someone choosing life and another person choosing death for the later generation. You, Mr. or Ms. The person reading this book, need to know the truth about the chain of events that seem to be happening at a natural flow in your life. And so, the battle for the coming soul begins.

A lot of times people come together for various reasons. If ordered by flesh and blood. But then there are times when people come together by the appointed will of God for the purpose of bringing another generation into the world. We see this in the Bible in Genesis 38. Although the situation was wrong, it served a greater purpose. My parents were married for 4 years. Long enough to have my brother and myself. I was the youngest. I was between 18 months and 3 years old when my parents separated. My mother made my brother and I go with my Dad, because out of 4 children, we were his.

Season 2

Now That You Are Here

Isaiah 43:1 But now thus says the Lord that created You, O Jacob, and He that formed You, O Israel, Fear not, for I have redeemed You, I have called You by Your name, You are Mine.

Jeremiah 1:5 Before I formed You in the belly, I knew You; and before You came out of the womb I sanctified You and I ordained You a prophet to the nations.

Look at the scriptures. There is a specific word in each scripture that will hopefully jump out at you. They are Redeemed in the first scripture and Sanctified in the second scripture. I am going to help you understand what these words mean by supplying definition. Stay with me, we're going somewhere.

The definition of Redeemed is :1. To buy back. 2. To free from captivity by payment of ransom. 3. To extricate from or help to overcome something detrimental 4. To release from blame or debt. 5. To free from the consequences of sin. 6. To change for the better.

The definition of Sanctified is: 1. To set apart to a sacred purpose or to religious use. 2. To set free from sin. 3. To make productive of holiness or piety.

I mentioned in the first section about a battle for the coming soul. For some of us the evidence of this battle might have started at the time of your birth. Consider any stories your parents might have mentioned, or someone might have said about your parents, relating to a complicated pregnancy, preterm labor, complications with organs not completely developed after birth. Maybe your parents were addicts and it was passed to you through blood. Any reason you had to stay in the NICU for any reason or had an extended stay at the hospital for further tests. The evidence of the battle for my soul was preterm labor, for one, I was born 5 weeks early. A second form of evidence was that when I was born, my lungs were not fully developed, and I had to stay in the NICU for a while. I couldn't go home with my parents. Looking back at that third definition of Redeemed. It states: To extricate from or help to overcome something detrimental. It's evident that my parents eventually were able to bring me home. As were yours. That portion of the battle was won in favor of the earlier generations that chose life and interceded for the future generations. And so, we're talking about when in life the evidence of the battle for your soul began.

As I shared, mine began at day 1. August 3, 1977. Others reading this book, the evidence of the battle for you might have been a little later. You might have gone through some horrific events as a little child that didn't kill you. It could have been molestation. It could have been rape. It could have been a bad car accident. It could have been accidently taking something poisonous. It could have been someone giving you too much medicine. Your parents could have had some drama going on and you were in harm's way. If you are reading this book, another point goes to the generation that chose life. But the battle is not over just because you overcame that. Some situations leave scars that are unseen. The situation of my birth or someone else reading this book, there might not have been any scars other than from surgeries. But we are about to talk about the scars that somethings leave on a spirit or the mind. And behavior.

Season 3

Just because there's no tangible evidence of a battle doesn't mean there isn't one

In the first section of this book I mentioned that almost a year or two after I was born, my parents got divorced and my mother made my brother and I go with my dad. Every battle is not physically tangible. During my early years of growing up I can't remember.

The reason for that is because however traumatic the situation resulting in my parents' divorce, it caused me to go into survival mode in my head. I blocked out. I remember only bits and pieces of times that my brother and I went to my mother's house on the weekends. I remember bits and pieces of going to daycare or starting school. The battle had become evident in my mind. Even though
I was with my dad most of the time. And I loved my dad. Still do. But being with my dad had nothing to do with the battle going on inside.

My dad remarried and had a baby with his wife. I still remember feeling disconnected somehow. I remember feeling like I was in a world that I wasn't supposed to be in. I remember more than anything, the last night my brother and I saw my mom. She was bringing us home from spending the weekend with her. My brother had told my mom that my step-mom had spanked him for something. When we got home, we came in the house and my mom charged up the stairs after my step-mom. She was hollering. My brother and I never moved from where we were standing. My dad went up the stairs behind my mom. He carried my mom over his shoulder back down the stairs. He hemmed her up on the front porch. I was so frozen by all that I had just seen. My mom left and we never went to her house anymore. We never saw her any more. The reality of it took some time to settle in. WE never talked about it. And my dad never talked about it. We just went on like it never happened. But describing these feelings to any one at such a young age is impossible when you don't know what it is that you are feeling or what to call it. I can remember the only time I felt peace was waking up in the middle of the night hearing my dad playing on his keyboard or singing along with a Winans' album. Then I would cry myself to sleep. I can remember feeling angry. I was mentally rebellious. I say this because I was smart in school, but I made grades that barely passed me. I remember my dad saying to me every report card period that he didn't understand how I could start the school year off so great and then not continue to do what I was more than capable to do. He would ask me if my work was hard. And I would say no. And he would say "Well then what is the problem?" I would say in response "I don't know." He would say, "What do you mean you don't know?" He would give me a lecture on something very significant, spank me, and make me do my homework.

At that age I didn't know how to talk to my dad about the things that I was feeling. I was afraid to talk to my dad. As I got a little older, my mouth got a lot sharper especially towards my brother and step-sister. To the point of making her cry by what I said to her that was so nasty and ugly. And I remember not feeling bad about what I said. I remember having dreams that I was falling and never landed. I woke up from one of those dreams so angry that I punched my sister so hard in her back it should have woke her up, but it didn't. And she didn't even say anything about it the next morning. I was depressed as a child. I can say what it was now that I have knowledge of it. I used to rock myself to sleep so hard hoping to rock myself out of the emotional state I was in.

I used to drink glasses of water till my stomach hurt. And continued to drink it after my stomach started hurting. Signs of depression. I remember being in Girl Scouts and it was that time of the year to sell cookies. I brought cookies to sell to my teacher, but she didn't want them. I opened the box and shared them with my friends. By the end of the day, the box was empty. My step-mom had already told me to bring the cookies that I didn't sell home. So I go home with no cookies. On the bus ride home from school, I'm trying to come up with a story to explain these disappeared cookies. Maybe she won't even ask about them. Not likely. We always got home from school before my step-mom did. So when she walked in the door I was at the dining room table doing my homework. She asked me and my sister about the cookies.

My step sister had hers on the coffee table already. And I had an empty box. "Where are the cookies?", she asked. My response came out like it was something that happened every day. "My teacher shared them with me."

I'm laughing about this now. But it truly isn't funny. My step-mom was not convinced. Not by a long shot. She asked me my teacher's name, pulled out the phone book. She found her number and proceeded to call her. I'm praying that my teacher didn't pick up the phone. She did. My step-mom hands me the phone and tells me to tell her again what happened to the cookies. I continued with the same lie as before. Even arguing with the teacher. Like she was wrong. My step-mom ends the call with my teacher. I was in a lot of trouble. I got the beating of my life from her. And was going to get another one from my dad when he got home. I had never had a bruise before. But that day I had a lot. From the inside out. I tried to prepare myself for the one I was going to get from my dad, but he had gotten a phone call and had to leave. I guess I was safe. Why did I do that? Why did I lie? Fear. Fear of getting in trouble for not selling the cookies in the first place. I never tried to sell them. The end result was to write an apology letter to my teacher. I was so afraid of embarrassment from my teacher that I slid it on her desk when she wasn't in the room. I didn't even want to think about it anymore. Definitely didn't want to talk about it. I was purposely rebellious at school. Telling my teacher that I needed to go to the restroom, she would say not right now, and I just got up and walked out. By the time I got home My step-mom would have received a call from the school and she asked me what happened. I told her. She kept me from getting in trouble with my dad. I was restricted to my room a lot. And I was ok with the isolation. Here I was thinking that I was the only one having issues, my brother was also having issues. I can remember one time being home and realizing that my brother wasn't there. I looked all over the house for him. Even outside. He wasn't anywhere to be found. That was not like my brother. We always knew where each other were. All of us. Because for the most part, we were always together. Some time went by and he still didn't show up. I thought he might have been with my dad, until my dad shows up without him. My dad leaves to go find my brother. Now I'm worried, scared and feeling alone. How was I going live without my brother. He was the only connection I had left to my mom. If he left, I would have no one. There was something about me and my brother having the same mom and dad that made my mind process something different. At that age(around 8-9-10) I felt like we were all we had. My mom would call on our birthdays, and send us birthday cards. I remember my mom asking me what I wanted and I told her $20 all in ones. One day my dad was coming down the stairs counting these dollars. I was happy because I just knew that they were mine. But he never gave them to me. He never said anything either. I tried to correct myself by thinking maybe they weren't mine. But deep inside, I could never shake the feeling that they were. I just wanted my mom. I would cry a lot at night because I wanted her. When she would call, we couldn't stay on the phone long because we had to keep the line clear in case my parents called from work. At times the emptiness was gone, only to reappear whenever she called or whenever her niece came by the house. The first worst day of my life was the day my cousin told us that my mom had moved to Texas. She never said goodbye. I truly didn't know how to take that. She never said goodbye. That was the start of abandonment issues. I never liked good byes after that. Because to me it meant that I was never going to see that person again. Years passed and now I'm 12 and starting Junior High. My attitude is nasty. A decision was made that I was going to live with my mom in Texas, after a weekend when I didn't come home from school. I showed up at the house when I thought my dad was gone to work. My younger brother let me in. I went up the stairs to my room and my dad is coming out. My dad doesn't look like my dad. Some words were spoken and I laughed. In the process of laughing like I

was being smart, my dad slaps me so hard I fall to the floor. I was so stunned.

My dad had never slapped me. That changed everything. Any time my dad made a move, I was jumping. I was flinching. Now I just wanted to stay out of his way. I wanted to leave. There is something that needs to be understood. The severity of these battles doesn't always accommodate any particular age. But God doesn't allow you to go through more than what He knew you were strong enough to handle. You will understand better as you continue to read.

And there is something else I want to point out about my mom leaving me with my dad. My dad's blood line was the line that chose life.

Somewhere along my mom's blood line didn't. See how God was true to His word about Redeeming? That's just the beginning. So, if you ended up in what you can look back on now and consider it a safer place, You were under God's covering. But being in a safer place doesn't always mean that's where you will stay. Or where you need to stay.

Season 4

Moving To The Unknown

Genesis 12:1-3 Now the Lord had said unto Abram, Get thee out of thy country, and from thy kindred, and from thy father's house, unto a land that I will show thee. And I will make of thee a great nation, and I will bless thee, and make thy name great; and thou shall be a blessing: And I will bless them that bless thee and curse him that curseth thee: and in thee shall all families of the earth be blessed.

Again, my behavior reached a certain point, and my dad was all exhausted out of punishments. Him and my mom decided that I was going to live with her. I was born in Minneapolis, MN. My mom had moved out of the state some years back. She was living in Fort

Worth, TX. And that is where I went. At the age of 12. Remember I stated earlier that being in that physical safe place meant that you were under the covering of God.

You are probably thinking, why would God, who is intentional allow me to move out from under the covering? Let's find out. Remember in the second section we defined two words.

Redeemed and Sanctified. One of the scripture references was Jeremiah 1:4. Let's go back over the definitions and Jeremiah.

Jeremiah 1:5 Before I formed You in the belly, I knew You; and before You came out of the womb I sanctified You and I ordained You a prophet to the nations.

The definition of Sanctified is: 1. To set apart to a sacred purpose or to religious use. 2. To set free from sin. 3. To make productive of holiness or piety.

We see by the definition that God had set me apart for a sacred purpose. He established this purpose from my mother's womb. In other words, to answer the earlier question about why would God move me from the physical covering? God placed a covering on me from the womb. And if you are having the pleasure of reading this book, He did the same thing to you. So, when He moved me from Minnesota to Texas, I didn't lose the covering. Sometimes staying in a safe place, whether it be physical, or mental, even spiritual can hinders us. We can't grow staying in the safe place. We become comfortable and don't want to do anything else. We become afraid of the unknown, so we plant our feet where we are. In order for God to get the Glory out of your life, especially when He has chosen you for something, there comes a time where He has to move you. My time to be moved was at 12 years old. Staying with my dad would have hindered me. Using a Bible reference to back up what I am saying, we see in Luke 2:40-49 That at the age of twelve Jesus was in the temple preaching and teaching. The difference between Jesus

and myself and you are that you and I were not aware of our purpose on earth as Jesus did. But we shall all soon find out. Stay with me.

Season 5

A Sojourner in a Foreign Land

Genesis 23:4 I am a stranger and a sojourner with you: give me a possession of a burying place with you, that I may bury my dead out of my sight.

Stranger – 1. Foreigner 2. Intruder 3. A person with whom one is unacquainted

Sojourn – to dwell in a place temporarily

Foreign – 1. Situated outside a place or country and esp. one's own country 2. Not connected, pertinent, or characteristically present

Culture – The customary beliefs, social forms, and material traits of a racial, religious, or social group

Shock – To strike with surprise, horror, or disgust

I moved to Fort Worth, TX to live with my mother. I was 12 years old. She had remarried, and my oldest brother and older sister where all present. My mom, sister, and brother came to pick me up from the airport. When we got to the house, my step-dad was not there yet. When he got home, my mom proceeded to introduce us, and she ordered me to call him Dad. I immediately rejected that thought and made sure to say something. I told her "I already have a Dad. He is not my Dad and I'm not going to call him that". She became angry with me. She fussed at me, I cried, then went back into the kitchen and apologized to him. Because that is what my mom made me do. That began a dislike for my mom. In my mind I thought" How could she make me do something like that? I don't know that man". In my heart and mind, I was still rejecting the whole notion. I missed my dad so much at that particular moment. I swore in my heart that I was never going to replace my Daddy with someone I didn't even know until that day. I went to bed angry, crying myself to sleep. Only to be woken up throughout the night by the sounds the house was making. I was afraid. There were a lot of things that I wasn't used to. I had to share a room with my sister. That was no problem. I missed my sister. I was inwardly fascinated at the fact that we were finally back together from being apart for so many years. She would catch me staring at her. I didn't mean any harm. I wasn't used to her. She got upset and snapped at me. "Stop staring at me", she would say. My sister was glad about me being her sister until I had to invade her space. She would do little mean things to me. For instance, I was in Middle School and she was in High School. I didn't have to get up as early as she did for school. She would turn the big light on in the bedroom and it would wake me up.

I was afraid to say anything to my mom because I was afraid of my sister. The hate emanated off her towards me. One night my mom and her husband went out for the evening, my sister was listening to a Walkman radio. I asked her if I could see it when she was done, and she snapped a No at me. I went into the living room and sat on the couch. My brother asked me what was wrong, and I told him what happened. He told me to tell my mom when she got home because my sister was doing something she wasn't supposed to be doing anyway. When my mom got home, I made sure that I told her. After that night the hatred that my sister had towards me grew more. I remember talking to my brother one night while cleaning up the kitchen, we were talking about her. I mentioned that she was mean, and that I hated her. I didn't know the meaning of hate. It wasn't a word that was ever used in my Daddy's house. My brother went back and told my sister what I said, and she was so angry she wanted to fight me but my brother told me to just stay locked in the bathroom until she left for school. I said earlier that there were a lot of things going on in my mom's house that I was not used to. Moving with my mom was a serious culture shock. I would go into the living room to watch television with my mom. I would sit down, lean over to her and give her a kiss on her cheek, tell her I loved her. She told me that I was being fake. Stop being fake, she would say. That threw me back. Why would she say that? I meant every word. I wanted to cry but held it in until I went to bed. Then the lights were off, and no one could see me. My brother had a habit of not coming home sometimes. I remember my step-dad's brother and nephew bringing him home. Later that night I would wake up listening to my brother getting a spanking. My brother and sister went at each other a lot. Meaning they argued.

They were spiteful to each other. Especially my sister. If you did something to her, she made you know that she was going to retaliate. My mom and step-dad argued. My mom would get a call from him, he was at work, she at home. She wouldn't want to talk to him, so she looks at me and tells me to tell him she's in the bathroom. I mentioned that she wasn't in the bathroom. If I lie, I'm getting in trouble. Why would she ask me to lie for her? She obviously felt convicted and never asked me again. She tried to be funny the next time and stood in the bathroom. Another shock was that my mom made going to church a choice. It wasn't a choice in my Dad's house. It was the way of life. Every Saturday my mom would ask my sister and I if we wanted to go to church the next day. I couldn't understand that, and it made me afraid for some reason. Not going to church? What are we going to do? Foreign. Shocked. My mom and Step- dad would go out without us. We later find out they were looking at houses. They find one and we eventually move. Between the time of my parents finding a new house and moving my older brother leaves and doesn't come home. He ends up going to juvenile and then to Brownsville, TX. So, I now I had my own room. That summer, my step- dad got sick and had to go to the hospital. I honestly was unfeeling about that whole thing. No, I take that back. I was mad at my mom because earlier that day she had called home from work barking at him to get up and go to work and he was telling her that he didn't feel good. He was having a very bad head ache. He got out of the bed after he had me call an ambulance. He stayed in the hospital for a few days. He couldn't go back to work for almost a month if I remember that right. My brother was only gone for 6 months. So, when we found out that he was coming home soon, I had to move into the room with my sister. And she made me sleep on the floor. My mom or step-dad asked about it and decided that we would rotate sleeping on the floor. But my sister always had a bad attitude so I just insisted that I was ok down there.

Going to church was still sporadic until I guess my mom got bothered enough in her spirit and then we started going more on a regular basis. I think it was because of a short story I wrote about a young girl who didn't go to church much. I showed it to my mom and she asked me was the story about me. I lied to her and said no but she knew I was lying. And she said that in front of everyone in the living room. My step-dad and sister. And as I was in the living room, they proceeded to make jokes about me. Something else I was not used to. Making fun of people was not anything we did in my dad's house. My feelings stayed hurt. They always made fun of me. The clothes that I brought with me from my dad's, to the way I talked, danced, ate. Positioned my hands. My step-dad bought me a birthday cake for my birthday, the next morning I hear my mom and sister talking about me while eating my cake. I stayed in my room a lot. My sister had a habit of always stealing the show. What I mean by this is, my mom and I could be having a conversation and my sister was in another room. She would come wherever we were and just start talking to my mom as if I wasn't even there. I was hurt because my mom was in fact acting like we weren't talking. I would just get up and leave the room. I felt that it was stupid to be fighting for my mom's attention. We were sisters. Remember the title of this season is A strange sojourner in a foreign land. One Sunday morning we went to church. At the end of the sermon, there was the alter call to accept Jesus Christ. I literally felt a push in the middle of my back and I stood up and went to the front. The next Sunday we went to church. After the sermon the alter call came again , as the other week.

Then there was a call for people who wanted to receive the Holy Spirit. Again, I felt that push in the same part of my back as the week before. I went forward. We were led out of the sanctuary into a room. There were about 5 women standing around me telling me to say Thank you Jesus really fast with their hands on my stomach. I was completely turned off. I couldn't concentrate. I went home from church without the Holy Spirit. Or so I thought. Later that night in my room alone, I got on my knees in front of my bed and prayed. I said "God I would really like to have Your Holy Spirit. Can I please have it?" I immediately heard a voice tell me to open my mouth and repeat after Him. I was speaking in tongues. I felt heat in my body. I was so excited. But not excited enough to tell my mom or anyone else. I felt good. I had a secret that I was keeping to myself. My mom made us get up in the mornings and pray and read our Bible before getting ready for school. I was happy about speaking in tongues in the privacy of my room. I honestly felt like I had something no one else in the house had. After receiving the Holy Spirit, it seemed that something changed. My sister became more vicious to me through her behavior. I was trying to do everything I could to let her know that I was a good sister and that she didn't need to treat me like that. I gave her anything and everything of mine that she wanted. She just tore it up. I gave her money one time to go with her friends and she said she was going to pay me back. I waited a long time but never said anything. One day my sister and brother were arguing about something and my brother asked her if she ever paid me back. She snapped No. She ended up giving me a bunch of coins in return for the solid bill that I gave her. My brother told her she was wrong for that. She just laughed. I just stayed quiet.

My mom started seeing another man and when the man would call, he would have to ask for my sister. That was evidently the only way the man was going to get any messages to my mom. The guy was a basketball player for a radio station and we got to go to a D.J. Quick concert. My mom seeing this man went on for a few weeks and then it was over as quickly as it started. And then something very unexpected happened one morning. Just as good as my step-dad left for work and we were up getting ready for school, my mom comes to my sister and I and tells us not to get on the bus after school because we weren't to come back to this house. My mom was leaving her husband. I was shocked. I was thinking, where were we going? My mom told us that she was going to be picking us up after school. I was still wondering where we were going, who was going to move our stuff? My mom was good at having escape plans. She came and got us from school and we were in a new apartment down the street from our school. My sister didn't seem as surprised as I was, which let me know that her and mom had already talked about it or this had happened before. And so there we were in a new home. My mind was still whirling. What was going to happen to us without this man here? Were my thoughts. I didn't know what to do. I'm now 14 years old and was stressed out about the situation. This was the third move for me in the three years. Moving to Texas in October of 89, moving to another house in May of 90, moving to the apartment in May of 91.

Season 6

How to go looking for something that you're too scared to talk about?

After all of the different forms of rejection from my mom and sister, I was feeling an emptiness inside. My whole little life living with my dad, I wanted my mom. Only to come to where my mom is just to be rejected by her. The addition of my sister's rejection made me feel even more empty and alone. I didn't have that many friends at school that I felt comfortable talking to. Alone and Empty. I began looking for something. Didn't know what it was, or even how to describe what I felt was missing in my life. But I was going to find it. I didn't know the first step. But I wanted to find it. My first year in high school was a little scary. I tried my best to be myself and stay out of my sister's way. I didn't want to run into her at school no more than she wanted to see me. She was still vicious. My mom leaving her husband kind of gave my sister and I some breathing room. So, to speak. That summer my sister was working and I was doing some babysitting for my mom's friend. My sister and I go to the mall and stay to long.

We miss the last bus. My sister calls our mom. I'm not sure what was said in the conversation. My mom and her boyfriend come to pick us up. When we get home, my mom is ready to jump on me. I wasn't shocked. Of course, my sister made the situation with missing the last bus, my fault. When it wasn't. There was a guy trying to get my attention in a store. I ignored him because I was trying to get to the bus stop. My sister insists that we have time, and encourages me to go over and talk to him. She said that she would let me know when we needed to leave. I wasn't with it at first but silly me, trusted her. Just to get jumped on when we got home. Such was my life. I didn't even argue about it. My mom was just going to believe my sister anyway. My sister was able to buy her new clothes for school because she worked. I, who was too young to work, didn't get new clothes for school. And now it's my second year in High School. My mom had a second job in the evenings which left my sister and I at home alone. My brother had been gone long before we left the last house. My sister would be on the phone with boys discussing coming over to see us before my mom was gone to her second job.

Within minutes of my mom leaving and making it to work, we were having company. And we made them leave 30 minutes before my mom got off work. Nothing was happening outside of just conversation. But one visit was different. A young man that I liked for a long time and at one point was my hidden boyfriend came over. We talked and got some things off our chest to each other. We ended up in my room and was trying to have sex, but he never penetrated. It hurt too bad. So, we just stopped. We sat and talked some more.

This time we talked about having a relationship. We went to the same school, my mom already liked him. He rejected me. That wasn't what he wanted. I was crushed on a totally different level of rejection than my mom and sister. Rejected by the one person that I had strong feelings for. I had a hard time with that. But I never talked about it with anyone. Not even my sister when she was being decent to me. Later that summer I was rejected again by another boy. I started my next year in High School feeling numb. You see all these couples walking together down the hall stealing kisses in between classes. The guy carrying her books. At Valentine's Day, all the flowers, candy, and balloons. I wanted that to be me. I wanted someone to give me a stuffed animal. Not just anybody, an upper classman. It was evident that they had money. But I didn't really care about money. I just wanted someone to pay as much attention to me as they did my sister. Mind you, I wasn't jealous of her in any way. Her standards about a guy were totally different than mine. I wondered how she was getting so much attention as vicious as she was. Maybe she was just that way to me. One person did give a stuffed animal and some candy. I was very happy.

Crazy I never thought to give that person a chance. They really liked me. And another person secretly sent me candy by his cousin. I didn't even know if I had ever seen the individual, until I found out he was in my ROTC class. I wanted someone to be in love with me. I just wanted to throw myself into my work and focus on getting good grades. But that didn't happen. A young man that went to Middle School with me and High School offered to walk me home.

He asked me what time my mom was going to be home. My mom no longer had a car because my step-dad took it back, so she was riding the city bus. We had time. My sister was somewhere. Not home. Me and this person tried to have sex and he did penetrate. I lost my innocence that day. When he left, I felt the emptiness get bigger because I knew he wasn't going to have anything real with me. I was feeling ashamed and stupid. And didn't realize that I was starting a ride on a train that was destined to wreck. Trying to find what I was looking for. I mean. Oh, and we were back to not going to church and my mom had another boyfriend. One day I was coming out of class and I was hemmed up by a boy kissing all over me, asking me to have sex with him, I said no. Another day I was leaving class and a guy I called friend asked me if I wanted to leave for a little while. I liked him. He was cool. We knew each other from church. I didn't have feelings for him, but I didn't think we were going to do anything either. I went back to his house and we sat and talked a little bit and then before I knew it, he was on me and I didn't stop. He made me feel something I had never felt before. I was thinking maybe he did like me. That wasn't saying anything. He was just more experienced having sex than the others I was with. After that I turned down everyone else who tried to come at me. I was just really sick of my behavior and still hadn't found what I was looking for. A couple of months went by and I found myself always wanting to go to sleep.

I was getting to school late because I just didn't feel like going. I wanted to go to In House suspension so I could go to sleep. My Math teacher, Ms. Burns pulled me to the side one day and asked me if I was pregnant. I was appalled. I asked her why would she

ask? She mentioned that my breast were looking a lot bigger than usual. I began to get scared and wondered if my mom noticed anything. Because I haven't said anything to her about how I was feeling. One day, I got home from school and my cousin called to talk to my mom, but my mom wasn't home. I asked her how can a person tell if they're pregnant. She asked me how I had been feeling, and I told her. She suggested to get it checked out. I asked her to please not say anything to my mom. She didn't. The next time I was at school, me and two of my friends left at lunch time to go take pregnancy tests. One of them knew of a pregnancy center that gave free tests. All three of us were curious if each of us were pregnant. We went in and took the test. We talked to the advisors that were there. While we waited for our results, we had to watch videos about abortions, as if that was even an option. At least it wasn't for me. I'm now 15 years old in this center waiting on the results of this pregnancy test. Positive. I was too outdone. How was I going to tell my mom this?! What is going to happen?! My sister walked up on me in the cafeteria talking to my friends about the test results and trying to check for double heartbeats. So now she knew. At the end of that day she tried to fuss at me about when I was going to tell my mom, so I could start going to the doctor. She threatened me. If you don't hurry up and tell her I will. She said. I was beyond scared. I was stressed out. I got in the tub at night rubbing on my stomach already in love with this little person that I didn't know yet. My sister kept pestering me about telling my mom until I finally decided when I was going to tell her.

I was scared to death. At 15 years old, you can't just so blasé tell your mom that you're pregnant. Not my mom. The day came for me to tell her. We were riding in the car and I told her that I had a hard test this week. I failed. She said what kind of test was it? I said a pregnancy test. I just knew I was going to just fall right through the seat in the car. I wanted to run, I wanted to hide. I wanted to wake up from the bad dream I was having. All she could say next was WHAT!!!!!! Another moment that I was feeling so alone. And that was just the start of it. When we got home, my sister asks her Did she tell you? I was even more stunned. I shouldn't have been. My sister always got a kick out of telling on me and watching me get in trouble. But I was stunned just the same. She had already told her. I felt betrayed. I wanted to cry. I wanted to scream. I felt double teamed once again. Alone. Another week or so later I came home from school and saw pamphlets on the coffee table to an adoption center. I was so mad. I was not giving up my baby. I was ready to go to work just to take care of my own baby. I was to young my mom said. I was determined that I was not giving up my baby. No way!!!! My brother called me a sneaky little devil. I was looking at him like Why would you say that to me? I was so tired. I just wanted to be able to do everything for myself and not need anyone's help. I was exhausted with always wanting to hide in my own skin. My mom took me to go apply for Medicaid, so I could start going to the doctor. Out of nowhere a lady that went to the same church as we did started coming around and she and her daughter took me shopping to get some clothes that I could wear while I was pregnant. They took me to the grocery store a lot to get fruit and other stuff. I went and applied for WIC. And then I also made another friend from the same church.

She was young and married and picked me up to spend some time with me. I was always afraid of opening up too much because I didn't want anything getting back to my mom. The nice lady that showed up out of nowhere, she had not long ago went through the same thing with her daughter. She would come get me and let me spend days at a time at her house. Giving me a break from my mom is what she said. I still wasn't able to open up. Still scared. Her daughter was nice and I told her somethings making her promise not to tell even her mom. I'm sure she told her mom everything and they just wouldn't tell my mom because I was scared. My step-dad found out probably by my mom and he gave her the car back. Going back to school after the results came out was very awkward. Boys were making snide remarks. One young man approached me, asking was it his. I was once head over heels for this idiot. I was repulsed by the thought. I told him, "Do the math and you tell me". I hadn't been with him in any time frame close to being pregnant. And I was thanking God for that. Even the ROTC teacher had something to say pertaining to letting the individual responsible go to college because that's where he was headed. I was flabbergasted by the approach. I was thinking "What about me?" I had approached the father of my baby with the news. I wanted to tell him myself. He surprised me by not believing me. More rejection. I didn't want to go to school anymore because I didn't want to see his face. You don't believe me? Why would I lie? Other guys? There were no other guys around that time. The only peace I had was at night in the tub or in the bed feeling my baby move. That summer my mom made me change schools. I was kind of glad. For the escape. This school accommodated pregnant teens.

And we could see the Nurse Practitioner instead of going all the way to the hospital for doctor visits. Except for sonograms or something. My life was changing. I was starting to have really bad Charlie horses in my legs. They would hurt so bad. My mom would come and rub them out. That made the pain worse. But at this time such was my life. And always in the morning right before the school bus came. Climbing on the bus was hard. School itself was good. I had good teachers that cared about you and your condition. My 16th birthday came, and the nice lady asked me what I wanted. I told her a coloring book and crayons. My mom made fun of me and talked bad to me for asking for such childish things when I was about to be a mother. I wasn't trying to stay a child. I was only too aware of what was happening to me. I needed stress relievers. Coloring relaxed me and put me in a zone that did not include my mother or sister. Getting close to eight months pregnant, my mom decides to move again. And this time without my sister.

Season 7
Too Much Too Fast

The day comes for us to move into another
apartment. This changes some things. I had to
get a new pick up address to keep riding the bus
to school. Where we moved to was considered
another ISD. Another change was that my step-
dad was coming back around. He wasn't there
every day, yet, but he would come take me to
school and stuff like that. Then he and my mom

were into it again and he would disappear. The moment I felt my baby trying to come out, we were headed to the hospital. An 8 lb. 10 oz girl. I was so happy. During my earlier months of pregnancy, I would daydream of what she would look like. She was beautiful. She was mine and I loved her. I had a hard time adapting to the changes of my body without the baby inside. What was going to happen now? The one thing that I was never concerned about was my instincts to taking care of my baby.

Earlier we talked about unseen battles that go on. Well now that I was home with my baby, the battles came. I was hearing voices in my head that were telling me to throw my baby across the room.

I had heard the doctors and everyone refer to post-partum-depression, but didn't know what it looked like. I didn't think I was depressed any more than I already was. My mom doted on my daughter all the time when she was home. Some people would think that she was being helpful, like letting me rest. And keeping her all the time. The proud grandmother, right? That wasn't the case at all. Appearances was everything to my mom. When she didn't want to be bothered with her, she made sure to just lock herself in her bedroom. I'm left feeling confused. She never wanted to leave my own baby with me, until she didn't want to be bothered. And that made me feel small. What did she think I was going to do to her? Any little peep my baby made, my mom jumped and got her. I was feeling like, is this my baby or yours? Whenever I did something that my mom thought was wrong, she would threaten to take my baby away. I would cry, and she would just look at me really evil like. I didn't think the mistake was so major that she had to go to that extreme. I was a brand new mom. Why not try to help me? She wasn't letting me be her mom. She would constantly take over and make me look like I wasn't doing things right. That depression was deepening. Whenever I would leave and go to the nice lady's house or hang with her daughter, I started to open up about somethings. I felt like everything I was holding in was going to burst out of me. One day my mom made the mistake by running her mouth to the lady about her threatening my parental rights, and the lady defended me. She told my mom to never say that to me again. That was mean. She told her I was trying. My mom wasn't trying to help me, so I was learning things as I went along. My daughter was now 2 weeks old. My mom gets up and walks in to my room where my baby was, stands over her crib and says in a low evil voice, "I am not going to pay for one more thing in this apartment by myself." She looked up at me and then down at my daughter.

She says "It would be a shame for my grandbaby to grow up knowing her grandmother killed her mother." I felt like somebody had just blew me in to a wall. Did she just say what I heard her say? She wants me dead, so she could have my baby!!!!! Kill me?!!! So I say "Did you just threaten my life?" She looked at me with this evil smirk on her face. I lost all respect for her that day.

I never looked at her the same again. I told her that I wanted a job when I found out I was pregnant, but she wouldn't let me. She said you were pregnant and not old enough. But you aren't pregnant anymore and old enough now. So, I got myself together and prayed that I found a job that day. I was scared that she would have tried to carry out what she wanted to do. But I was ready to fight no matter what. She was even more my enemy. The first place we went to hired me on the spot. Praise God. I will be able to live to see another day. I had to go get an ID and I had my SS card. God was really looking out for me. I was grateful. I was now working. Christmas came, and we were to go over to the nice lady's house. That morning after my mom got off the phone with her, she had a call from my sister and they proceeded to talk really nasty about the nice lady. I was hurt. This lady has helped my mom a lot to be able to deal with having not just one teenage daughter but two. That's right, my sister was pregnant before we moved. But my mom told her she couldn't move with us. This lady helped so much. They were so wrong in the way they talked about them. The lady and her daughter. I had had enough of the mean stuff. I had to tell them how my mom and sister were treating them. We were ready to go now. The daughter came and got me, and the baby and the nice lady was coming to get my mom. That was my opportunity to tell her.

I begged the daughter to the point of crying not to tell her mom until after we went home. We stayed overnight at their house. I couldn't sit by and let my mom and sister act fake. My spirit was so uncomfortable. After that day the nice lady barely talked to my mom anymore. The daughter would call periodically to check on me and the baby and I couldn't talk freely because my mom was in my mouth asking what was being said. I was always a bad liar. Meaning, even I didn't believe what I said, I know my mom didn't. My mom now had a new friend from work. She was invited to visit their church.

The lady came and picked up my mom and my baby. I didn't go because I had to work. I was also back in school off maternity leave. I was working, going to school and taking care of my baby. My mom made sure that every time I got paid I took out for my tithes, daycare fees(my baby went to the daycare at school), diapers and wipes for 2 weeks, and bus fare(I had to ride the city bus to school now). Everything else, I had to give to my mom. It wasn't a problem except I didn't make a lot or work a lot at first, because I was a student. I had to fix this. I never had anything for myself. Even the money I gave my mom, she would just spend it on my daughter. Well I could have done that myself. I look up one day and my step-dad is moving in. I said too much too fast. And now we are all attending this new church. My mom taught Sunday School. Something she always enjoyed doing. And always made a habit of making me the teacher's pet.

I never wanted to be her pet. I wanted to blend in with everyone else in the class. But other than that, I would always enjoy the service. I always felt something there.

Not realizing that the fire of the Holy Spirit was flaring up inside of me because I was around like kind. I'm still a sojourner here. Every sermon talked right to my parents. No doubt. Things were changing more. My parents made me quit my job, because they found out that there was a young man at work that liked me. And we were kind of sneaking around on the job. I remember when I first started the job, I told my mom about a guy that asked to take me out. She said "Why you?" with this sneer on her face. I was stunned by the question and the tone in which the question was asked. I wanted to ask "What's wrong with me?" But I just walked out of her bedroom asking myself, "What's the use?" My mom was becoming more unbearable to be around at home, so I asked my shift manager to schedule me for work every day if she could. My co-workers had front row seats to my embarrassment.

Some of them would get upset about the way my mom was treating me. I was trying to take care of my daughter. Why would they treat me like such a child about this? My grades started falling at school. I was having thoughts of quitting school just to work. Working was my escape. And then I thought about what my daughter would think if I didn't finish school. I wanted her to be proud of me walking across the stage. My mom's threat of killing me stayed in the back of my head. The hate that I was starting to feel towards her was getting bigger. But I never acknowledged the feeling for what it was. But the truth is that it really was hate. And withdrawal. My parents were evidently tired of me not working so I went out and got another job. Hired on the spot again. Praise God. But I was angry because they were making me look like I couldn't keep a job and it was my choice to quit the last one when it wasn't. It wasn't fair.

When I wasn't working, I wasn't speaking to my mom. I literally had nothing to say. We could both be in the same apartment and I never say anything. I had not even spit for her for real. She would get mad because I wasn't talking. We argued a lot. My step- dad had to intervene a lot. He told her to stop taking my money, so I could better take care of my baby. My mom was livid. She had to control everything. I would be in the bathroom sitting on the toilet, crying, after giving my daughter a bath and getting her ready for bed. And my daughter would wipe my tears. Whenever I would pat her back, walking around with her, she would be patting mine. I knew she loved me. If no one else did.

Another change was shortly on the way. My sister was pregnant with her second baby and living in her own place. Evidently there had been conversation about the hardships my sister was having, paying her bills and such. My mom tells her she can move in with us. I didn't understand it. Why? And not again. My mom tells me to make room for my sister's belongings. I did. I put my stuff on the right. In my bedroom closet. And in the bathroom. I was going to give myself the better side. I was here first this time. My mom made me move my stuff over. She wants the right side. It really didn't matter about the sides. I was angry because once again it's all about my sister. I couldn't catch a break.

My step-dad didn't want me hanging out with my sister. I guess he thought her behavior would rub off on me. He didn't know me well. I have my own mind. The pastor at the church was a college professor. He let me know that the college was offering a scholarship to students who wanted to pursue a career as a teacher. He let me know that in order to be considered for the scholarship I had to submit an essay about why I wanted to be a teacher. I wrote a draft, he proof read it and submitted it for me. I was going to be on my way to college. I sent off to different colleges for information about their campus. One stipulation to the scholarship was to go to the Junior College for two years and then finish at a four-year college. So that is why I sent off for information. I wanted to go to college. I wanted to graduate from High School, so my daughter would be proud of me. Getting through the last year of school was so hard. And it wasn't anything about school that made it hard, it was the mess going on at home. I was starting to feel alive when the pastor began to help me. I was so happy about the thought of going to college for something I have always wanted to do. And the possibility of finally being acknowledged as an individual.

Being in my own place and taking care of my daughter without my mom was making me happy. My happiness was about to be short lived. More changes. My parents go to have a meeting with the pastor and his wife. And they were taking a lot of books. I don't know what the meeting was about until they came back. My mom had stepped down from teaching. Why? I knew why. The Holy Spirit told me. Now what? Well my step-dad and I were still on the praise team and such. He was also starting to grow in his faith. He accepted his call to preach. And one Sunday night service, he did. It didn't make me feel the same as when my own dad would preach. But I was still proud of him. That was the first and last time, because shortly after that, the decision was made that we were all leaving the church. But we didn't leave right away. But the distance was growing. Every time I would mention the pastor or his wife, my parents would be evil and ugly in their comments towards them. I asked my step-dad about buying me a class ring for graduation. He says, "Ask Pastor----". I felt the jealousy. It was wrong. The man was just trying to help me become independent. What was wrong with that? The pastor was wanting to help me apply for housing. He was putting his mom's house on housing and was going to make sure that I got into it. On the way to school one morning my mom asked, "What does your income have to be to get on housing?" She asked knowing that I didn't have an income. I answered, "Nothing I guess if they're going to give it to me." The comments and attitudes were just wicked. It always made me nervous because I never knew how my mom was going to act from one moment to the next. Literally. I can remember one evening out of nowhere, my mom went outside. She comes back in with a pretty thick branch and thought she was going to whoop me with it. She was saying that she was tired of my behavior. What?! Really?! I was tired of her behavior. It was crazy. I started praying for God to just protect me and my baby. One day I remember making a decision that me and my daughter were just going to leave. By this time my parents were acting like they didn't want us here. I got the clues. And I was still waiting to hear back about the scholarship. I had gotten an invitation to attend an orientation at the Community College in a week. So this day I call my cousin and ask him to come get me and my daughter. He came and we drove around for a long time. I finally asked him why such a long drive?

He wanted to make sure that I was sure about what I was doing. I was. So I went to my friends house. We stayed the weekend. We went to church on Sunday and after church, the pastor called a meeting with me and my parents.

I was upset by all of the fakeness. I charged my mom up about wanting to take my baby. They were making me look stupid. I was pissed off. Empty promises were made and we all went back home. I just knew it was not going to last long. Every time someone came into our lives to help us in one way or another, my mom would always do something to separate. The only allies I had were gone. Time rolls on, and I have changed jobs again. Now I'm a waitress working until late at night. My mom was again all too happy to keep my daughter. My mom was throwing out false accusations in reference to me never being at work at night, but out with some guy. Sometimes I wished to have a date. But by this time the comment my mom made before conditioned my mind to think it will never happen anyway. Then another time I came home from work and spoke to my parents. It had been raining on the walk home. The blouse I was wearing was a little wrinkled from me trying to cover myself. My step-dad asked me about my shirt being wrinkled and I told him the truth.

My step-dad was mad at me for like a whole week. I didn't even know. And you can always tell when he was mad about something, because he would walk around like a big iceberg. Just freezing, frosty air blew off of him.

It disturbed everyone's peace in the house. So I knew he was mad but I didn't know that he was mad at me. My parents were mad at each other, again. While they were having an argument after church, I heard my mom say, "She doesn't even know why you're mad at her". I was like, What? Mad at me for what. Immediately the Holy Ghost reminded me about the night it rained and the wrinkled blouse. He also thought I was out doing something that I wasn't. Another change was shortly on the way. My sister was pregnant with her second baby and living in her own place. Evidently there had been conversation about the hardships my sister was having, paying her bills and such. My mom tells her she can move in with us. I didn't understand it. Why? And not again. My mom tells me to make room for my sister's belongings. I did. I put my stuff on the right. In my bedroom closet. And in the bathroom. I was going to give myself the better side. I was here first this time. My mom made me move my stuff over. She wants the right side. It really didn't matter about the sides. I was angry because once again it's all about my sister. I couldn't catch a break.

My step-dad didn't want me hanging out with my sister. I guess he thought her behavior would rub off on me. He didn't know me well. And now we have left one church and started going back to a previous church. The whole time my sister was staying with us, every night they gave her the blues because of her situation. I would come home from work and she was coming from they're room with her face all red from crying. Again this was happening a lot. What in the world? The arguing continues between my parents, so my mom plans to get an apartment with my sister and leave me and my step dad. I didn't know this at the time. Somehow or another my mom wasn't able to get the apartment with my sister. My sister ends up moving out. So my mom is back to acting like she's in love with my step-dad. I start seeing moving boxes. It looks like something is about to happen real fast. I go to work and call my uncle. My step-dad's brother. I explain to him what is going on and ask him if me and my daughter could come stay with them. They haven't said anything to me about moving and I want to make sure that my baby and I have somewhere to go. He told me that surely, they wouldn't just leave without me. I wasn't comforted by anything he was saying. I later find out the reason why my mom and my sister didn't move together because my sister told me. She was mad at my mom. And now gone. All I ever had to do was wait for my mom and sister to get mad at each other and my sister would tell me all I needed to know. My thoughts were, You were already in your own place, why would you give it up to come over here with her anyway. You know how she is better than I do.

So that explained my mom's sudden change in behavior towards my step-dad. She needed something from him. This fake, hypocrite, liar. The numbness grew even more. This pattern of behavior is disgusting. Manipulation is something my mom was crafted in. It worked on everyone else but me. So here we are the moving day. And they still haven't said anything about it to me.

I had talked to my uncle again the day before the move. He tells me to go ahead and pack my stuff anyway. What was I supposed to do if they say I wasn't going with them? I was lost. But I did what he said and packed. When they loaded up the truck, so did I. But I was scared. I didn't know what was going to happen. We drove down the street to the new apartment. I'm so scared I'm almost sick to my stomach, riding in the back of this truck.

Season 8
Getting Pushed Out

Being at that other church gave me something I didn't know I was crying out for. I was crying out to a stronger source that I totally forgot about. My spirit was crying out to God. I thought He was gone. But being at that other church and the things that I was feeling let me know that He wasn't. That night when we had finished unpacking the truck, my mom tells me not to unpack my stuff. She said, "Don't unpack your stuff." I didn't know what to feel at that point. I remember sitting on the couch wanting to cry but nothing was coming out. I had to figure something out. What was she saying? I couldn't stay? Where was I supposed to go? I sat on the couch waiting to see if she was going to come back and say anything else. She didn't. Everyone went to bed. I couldn't sleep. 17 years old and this is what's happening to me. Why? I got up the next day and walked on egg shells.

My step-dad was on vacation so he was home. He stayed in his room with the door closed most of the day. Then when my mom got home from work, she went directly to her room and closed the door. My daughter would stand at their door calling for them and they would never answer. This little girl that they doted on so much for such a long time and now they would hide from her.

I'm looking at my daughter and my heart is breaking. She doesn't know what's going on.

She's crying and screaming at their bedroom door and they never answered. That was so wrong. She didn't do anything wrong. She didn't deserve that from them. I took her outside. My daughter's dad stayed in an apartment right across the parking lot from us. He never saw us. But I would see him. Why didn't I ever say anything to him? Afraid. We weren't in school anymore. Anytime I took my daughter out during the day, I would run into other guys from school. They would look at my daughter and shake their heads knowing who her dad was. There was a park across the street from the apartments we lived in. I took her there and let her play until she got tired. She loved the park. When we got back, my parents would always start drilling her about where she had been. Who was your momma meeting up with? I told them that I took her to the park. They didn't believe me. My step-dad asked me who I went over there to see. Nobody. I took her to the park because you guys were in your room and she was crying. WE usually have to make you take her out. That was a lie. They usually had her all the time. I'm looking puzzled because I know they were lying. But I couldn't say that to them. On my step-dad's birthday, I take my daughter to my job and we have lunch. Just me and her. I go pick up a couple of birthday cards for him and then we come back. I slide the cards under his bedroom door. He never said thank you. My mom comes home from work and tells me that I have to find someone else to watch my daughter while I'm at work. I was shocked a little bit because I never had to find anyone else to do anything for me. My mom made sure that I always had to depend on her.

She thought that she was pulling a rug out from underneath me. But I actually went to God about the situation. I just told her ok. So, the next day I called the nice lady, who is also my daughter's God mother, and asked if she could watch her for me. I also let her know that I needed her to pick me up for work and then bring my daughter back when she picked me up and brought me home. I told her that my mom is making me find another baby sitter. She agreed to watch her. My mom came home for lunch the next day. She ate a sandwich and said we needed to get ready to go when she left. So, I grab my baby and her shoes and my money because I'm thinking that we were going to my mom's job with her. We get down to the car and she lets herself in and not us. She looks at me like what are you doing? She puts the car in reverse and then drives away, telling my daughter that she loves her. I was livid.

She made us leave with nothing. No clothes, no pullups for my daughter. Nothing but what we were wearing. Good thing it was the summer time and not raining. But it was still hot. I immediately went into survival mode. I walked my daughter across the street to the 7-Eleven, got some pull-ups and a perm and called a cab. I went to the pastor's house. They weren't there when I got there but their son was. And he was on the phone with one of their daughters that I was friends with. I told her about the situation and she said that we could come stay with her for a little while. She told me to stay and talk to her parents and she was coming to pick us up later. I stayed and talked to her parents. Then my daughter and I left to go to my friend's apartment. I felt a little better but I knew that this was only for a short time. The pastors went and talked to my parents. I don't know what was said but I was able to come back and get some things for my daughter and I while we stayed with my friend. We stayed for about a week.

Then we were told that we needed to go back home. I talked to the pastors again because I knew my mom was not going to hear it. I had to quit my job because I no longer had a place to stay. So, I'm jobless and homeless. This is what I'm telling the pastor and his wife.

So, they decide that they are going to take us back to my parents. But they were going to talk to them. It's late in the evening, so by the time we get there my daughter is asleep. My mom puts her in the bed and they all talk. The end result was that we were staying. But for how long?

Season 9

The Calm before another Storm

So, the end result as I stated earlier was that we were staying. The next month, being back with my parents was very awkward. I never knew when my mom was going to put me out again. And the even stranger thing about it was that she acted like what happened never happened. I can't even remember my 18th birthday. It went by that fast. I never got to walk across the stage for graduation. I asked my step-dad if he could go pick up my diploma. He went and picked it up. There, I had graduated high school. Hip hip hoorah. My mom came to talk to me about putting my daughter in daycare. She had wanted that before and even went and looked at one that she was interested in. Well, we now stayed across the street from this daycare that my mom loved so much. We go over and talk to the owners, we have a look around. My mom tries to ask me what I think about the place in front of the people, but I knew the decision was already made. She was putting my daughter here. And the plus side of this situation was that they were hiring for a floater. Someone who just came in half the day and helped relieve the teachers for breaks and helped during lunch time. I got that job.

Also, with me working there, the cost for my daughter being there became half off and was automatically deducted from my check. Praise God. My daughter was in daycare and I was working again. Even if it was part time. That quieted my mom for a little while. I worked at the Daycare for a couple of months and I hurt myself on the job. I came home and told my mom. She sent me back up to work to talk to the director about what happened. I asked her if they provided Workman's Comp for work related injuries. She told me that if I reported it, they were going to fire me. I didn't know how to respond to that, so I went back home and told my mom. She got upset. When I went to work the next day, they fired me. I asked if my daughter was still able to come and she said yes. What she didn't say was that the price went back to regular price. So I saw another daycare that was hiring and went in and applied. They hired me, and I started the next day. The next day I go to drop my daughter off at the Daycare. I signed her in and walked out the door. Regular stuff. Before I could get back in the car, the director is walking my daughter out of the daycare telling me she couldn't stay. I couldn't miss work and my mom had to go to her own job, so I just took my daughter to work with me. I walked in and explained the situation to my boss and she said she could stay until I could do something different. I was a toddler Teacher and I was not very good at it. But I did my best. My lunch break was 2 hours. I needed something. I called an old guy friend of mine. I wasn't even sure if his number was still the same. I was glad it was. He came and picked me up, and we went to this old empty house. We had sex. He did everything that he knew I liked. We were together for a short time in high school but lost track of each other.

He made me feel so good that I forgot about the problems I had going on outside of this empty house. But when it was time to take me back to work, I was feeling cold and empty. Like that house. At the end of that day I was fired. I said I wasn't good at being a toddler teacher. When my mom came and got me from work, I told her they let me go. She asked me why and I just shrugged. She assumed it was because of the short notice of having to bring my daughter that day. And I let her think that. I was still trying to hold on to the feelings that I had felt earlier that day with my friend. But they were quickly, speedily slipping away. I'm back at square one. The next day my mom calls me from work and tells me to get dressed she was coming to get us at lunch time. And to make sure that my daughter was looking extra cute. She even told me what to dress her in. I assumed that she wanted to show off my baby as usual. So, when we got to her job she lets me know that the McDonald's was hiring. She offers to walk around with my daughter while I fill out the application. And ask for hours that work around mine She said. I filled out the application and that was that. We went home at the end of her work day. The nice lady wanted to get my daughter for the weekend and I was fine with that. On Saturday I had an interview at McDonald's and was starting work the next Wednesday. I had to figure out who was going to watch my baby. My mom and I tell my step-dad about the new job. He suggests his niece to watch my daughter. I was comfortable with that. I didn't have any reason not to. My mom was trying to find herself inconvenienced by trying to figure out how much earlier she was going to have to get up and leave for work. I was disgusted as usual. She always sets something up and then when it looks like a go she got some reason why she is no longer in agreement.

She made me sick. So, we called his niece and she was cool with it. She watched my daughter for a little while and then my mom found another daycare.

She wasn't going to tell the niece. Which was wrong. I had to because that was my baby, and I felt like that was the right thing to do. What if I needed her again? Her excuse for finding another daycare was because whenever we dropped off my daughter at the niece's house, my daughter would start screaming at the top of her lungs and my mom didn't want to leave her there. Of course, I couldn't tell the niece that. So, my mom told me to make up a lie. I told her that since my daughter was used to be in a learning environment my mom wanted her in one. Yeah. I'm working at McDonald's for a while and one of my sister's co-workers is eyeing me. We start talking for a little bit and then my sister lets me know that he was playing me. Then there is another young man who would come in and order the same meal every time. He would get his food, sit down and watch me. And then there was an older guy who would come in and admire for a while and then order food. The younger guy finally gave me his phone number. My mom knew about the guy that was playing me. We had talked about it. And she was glad when I wasn't talking to him anymore. But this young man, she didn't know about. And neither did my sister. The older guy was just that. I had no thoughts of anything with him. At least that's what I thought at that time. I was enthralled with tall, dark, and mysterious. So, Mr. Tall, dark and mysterious finally decided to give me his phone number. I called him on my day off. I called him at church on Wednesday nights working in the nursery. Well one evening he decides to return my call at my home. My mom and I had some words because it was a boy and she told me to get out.

It was cold and snowy around this time. I had no shoes on and no coat. My step- dad comes home and lets me back in. He has a talk with me about him getting ready to start driving trucks and he needed me and my mom to be alright while he was gone. I let him know that it wasn't going to be because of me. He knew how she was. Another argument happened and she tells me to leave. And for the last time.

Season 10

From the Hot Pan Into The Fire

Manipulate – To influence with intent to deceive

Mental – Of or relating to the mind

Emotional – Of or relating to emotion

Thief – One that steals esp. secretly

Rape – A carrying away by force

Ecclesiastes 3:8 A time to love, and a time to hate; a time of war, and a time of peace

After my mom told me to get out, I called my sister. She came and picked my daughter and I up, with our stuff this time. My sister told me that she had been discussing my situation with a co-worker/friend of hers. The co-worker/friend let my sister know that if I ever needed a place to stay, I was welcome to come.

So that is where I went. I was still working at McDonald's and my daughter was going to daycare. I had a ride to work daily and if I got off in time with the co-worker/friend, I had a way to go pick up my daughter. One day at work I had a visit from the older guy, he wanted me to come see him at his work area on my break. I did. He asked me how I was doing, and we talked about nothing. I was totally caught off guard when he asked to take me out and if this weekend was ok. I was wide eyed. He proceeds to tell me how he had been watching me, which I knew, and how he was captivated by my smile. He wanted to take me out. I said ok. That night I told the co-worker/ friend about the encounter and asked her what she thought I should do. She said whatever you want. I'll watch your daughter for you. I said ok thank you. The next day at work I let him know when and what time to pick me up. The end of the day was a shocker. I got off later than usual and had no way to pick up my daughter before the daycare closed. I panicked. I called the co-worker friend and couldn't get an answer at first. I then started blowing up Mr. Tall, dark and mysterious' phone. He had a car. I mean I blew it up. I needed help. I finally got a hold of co-worker/friend and I asked her if she didn't mind picking up my daughter. She didn't mind. I immediately called the daycare and told them who was picking up my daughter. I was partly relieved. Now I just needed a way home. I proceeded to blow up his phone again until I got an answer. I thought he was still at work here in the hospital. He wasn't. He said he would come get me. I walk outside to wait for him and co-worker/friend was pulling up. I started walking towards her car to get in it. I was tired of waiting on Tall, Dark and Liar, at this point. But right when I was getting into the car, he pulls up.

I was still about to leave with friend, but she told me to go with him and just talk to him. He did keep his word after all. I was irritated but I went with him. He took me home. I said thank you. We sat outside and talked for a few minutes and then he left. I didn't know how to feel about him. He always had my mind whirling. I never knew what to expect from him. It was crazy, and I felt like he was having fun at my expense. He was always grinning like he knew something I didn't. The next day at work I noticed a co-worker that I hadn't seen before and was wondering where she came from. I don't remember how we started talking but next thing you know we were friends. At least based on the definition of friend that I thought. That Friday came, and the older guy came and got me. He took me to his house. We sat and looked at television for about 5 minutes, then he was taking my shirt off and walking me into a bedroom that had to be a child's room because of the bunk beds. When we were finished, he took me home and told me he wanted to see me again. I went into the house and co-worker/ friend was surprised I was back already. I was like yeah me to. I talked to her a little while, took a bath and went to bed. I was feeling undefined. A couple of weeks went by and me and Mr. Tall, Dark, and Mysterious finally hooked up. He was a little bigger than I was used to. So, it hurt a bit. I wasn't sure if that was supposed to feel good or not. I had heard that the bigger the guy, the better the sex. But I wasn't so sure about this right here. It was over, and I was secretly kind of glad. I eventually got fired from McDonald's for my drawer coming up short. Yes, I took it. I was following behind this new "friend". I had never stolen anything from work before. I hurried to get rid of the money. I paid the daycare and what was left was just change. I didn't take that much.

But it was still something I shouldn't have been doing. I started riding around a lot with this chick. She was a stealer. A petty thief. Meaning she would steal little stuff out of Family Dollar or somewhere like that. I would watch her and wonder if I would be able to get away with it like she did. I convinced myself to try it. My heart was beating so fast. Things began to no longer work out at the co-worker/friend's house and I had to find another place to go. I called my step-dad's niece and talked to her about the situation. She told me to talk to her mom. I did, and she said I could come if I didn't mind her house being full. I really had no choice. So that Friday one of her son's and the niece came and got me. My step-dad was the baby brother to this sister. She was the oldest and she had a set of twin sons, two daughters and another son who worked on cars.

Going forward I'm going to refer to the twin sons as Evil and Good. The Good twin was the one that came and picked me up. Him and I had talked for a few days on the phone while I was waiting for Friday to come. He had relationship issues with his children's mother. She ran away a lot. Right when I got there, she had been back for a few days. A week before I left co-worker/friend's house I had filled out an application to work for the hospital where the McDonald's was. I had finally heard back from them and had gotten the job. Moving in with these people was an experience. My aunt told me that since I was 18 and had a baby and a job, I was considered an adult and there was nothing that could be said to me about anything I chose to do. I really didn't know how to handle this freedom. I cussed like a sailor. That was just the beginning. Yes, to me that was huge when you have been in a house where no one cussed. Basically, I was starting to pick up the same spirits that were in this house with these people. Cussing was only one of them.

My aunt couldn't never remember my name and I felt like she should have. And I felt embarrassed. For the most part everyone was cool with me being there. The niece and I didn't have to talk on the phone anymore. We now lived in the same house. There was always a lot of people in the house. A lot of moving around. I had a hard time getting used to staying up so much later than I was used to. Everyone worked in the house except the baby son mechanic, the niece I was friends with, my aunt and the Good twin's baby momma. I had just started my job and had to make sure someone took me to work in the morning. So, I would have to get the baby son mechanic to take me. And then the niece and her mom or whoever would pick me up. My daughter no longer went to daycare because I couldn't pay for it anymore after leaving McDonald's, so the niece watched her. I was grateful and relieved that I no longer had to worry about who was going to watch her. It was a great relief to not have to hear my mom's voice about anything. Anymore. All the school age cousins went to the same schools and came to the same house every day after school. Then late into the night, they went home. I mentioned that this sister was the oldest. There was three more sisters and another brother beside my step-dad. That brother's kids were my age and older. I didn't see them much anymore since I wasn't going over to their house with my step-dad. I made a mental note that it was always dark in the house, even during the day. That was strange to me. One night I went through a rejection with Tall, Dark and Mysterious. I cried and wondered why he treated me like that. No one in the house really cared what I was going through. I tried to talk to them. They all had their own stuff going on. I went to sit outside. I was feeling alone again. The Evil twin comes outside to talk to me. I'm honestly asking him why this happened. I'm thinking because he's a man, he could explain what I was doing wrong.

Whatever he started to say or was saying, I went completely deaf. But then a quick turn of events. He starts to tell me how he used to notice me whenever I would come over with my step-dad, and how he thought I was pretty. And if he thought the family would accept it, he would make me his girl and I would never have to worry about the dumb stuff I went through with that little boy. The difference between the two of them was that Evil twin was a man and Tall, Dark, and gone at this point, was a boy. I needed a real man, he said. I was just trying to process that my cousin was trying to talk to me. Was this right? What is going on? What do I do? He stood up and started to walk off and told me to think about it. I sat outside for a little while longer really thinking about what just happened. Wrestling with the idea. Hearing this voice in my head say "it would be your little secret." When I went back into the house, everything didn't look like it did when I first moved in. I went to bed wondering how he would act if I said no. We were pretty cool right now. I hoped to not upset him. I went to sleep saying to myself, maybe he was just playing as usual and won't even remember it the next day. I hope he doesn't remember this tomorrow. The next morning before he left for work, he asked me if I needed any lunch money, and what time was I getting off. I told him what time I was getting off and before I could answer the question about the lunch money, he gives me $40. I'm like I don't think I'm going to eat this much. He said just keep it. You might need it later in the week. I never had a guy give me money before. Not even my step-dad. I went to work and tried to spend it all. Childish right? I didn't spend it all. He picked me up from work that day and he talked to me about the work he did at a metal plant and that sometimes if the work was slow, they would be sent home. Just in case I was wondering what he was doing there to pick me up.

He let me know that he let whoever was coming to get me know that he would do it instead. This type of innocent behavior went on for a little while. If he went and got something to eat or drink he would walk in the door and give me the drink. Claiming he was full. The drink was full like no one had ever touched it. The night came that he came and got me out of my bed. He walked me into his bedroom by the hand and started undressing me really slow. He's talking to me but I can barely hear anything he's saying because he was trying to be quiet. I vaguely heard "I've waited a long time for this." His voice was deep. While I was laying there, I was wondering what I was doing here. What do I think about him? I had never thought one way or another about him. So, I started thinking then, while he was all over my body making me feel things. Yes, I thought he was a nice looking guy. Sweet maybe when he wasn't teasing me. Maybe this could work. Maybe. Maybe? No, no, no, no this can't be happening. I'm not doing this again, It's not right. My body was so tired from the sex and my thoughts that I dosed off in his bed next to him. I thought I heard something and hurried to get up and get out. When I had gotten paid, I bought a pager. He didn't hesitate to ask for the number. I was still sometimes hanging out with the "friend "girl that I had. If he felt like I was gone to long, my pager would go off. I would call the number back thinking it was the niece about my daughter. But it was him. He would ask me when I was coming home. I was like whoa. That was a little out there for people to know because it was his younger niece that paged me for him. Now I'm wondering if he had told anyone about us. I was scared. I wasn't prepared to answer any questions. I told him whenever I got there. He asked me if he needed to come get me from where I was.

I'm like NO!!! I didn't want the "friend" to suspect anything because she knew him as my cousin. She was looking strange at me while I was on the phone. Who is that? I'll be there, I said. I'll wait up for you. No, no you don't have to do that. I want to make sure you get in. He said. That was a logical answer because once the door was locked, you had to bang on a window for someone to open the door. I got home, he let me in and he went straight to bed. I was like uh ok. So, I went to bed. A couple of days later it was announced that he was going back to a lady that he was once engaged to. He was only at his mom's because they were having problems. I'm pissed off. Yeah the emotion came as a surprise to me to. I didn't realize that I had come to have feelings for the Evil twin. We were sitting in the car waiting on some other people, we were going to get something from the corner store. I went off. Why do you have to go over there? Why can't you just stay here with me. What's the problem? You don't like me anymore? He didn't really say anything. I was like fine then. Go. And don't come back if she's who you want to be with. That night, really late that night, he came and woke me up, we went to his room like before. This time something was different. He tells me that he's scared. He's falling in love with me. I don't think the family is going to be ok with this. I was stuck with the "Falling in love" I was so stunned to hear him talk like this. I never would have taken him as the type of person to be honest and open about his feelings. But then again it was in the dark. That was the last night we were together like that, on good terms. As quickly as he said the words of being in love with me, they were replaced with something else. All of a sudden, he's not speaking to me. Not even teasing me like he was. No more giving me money, no more picking me up from work, no more even acknowledging me.

I was invisible as far as he was concerned. I remember trying to ask him for money for pantyhose or something and he snapped at me. I'm not giving you sh*t he said. I was like stop playing I need some stockings. Get it some other way. He gave me a dollar. I looked at it and asked "What am I supposed to do with this?" Then he called me a b*tch. I'm not giving you nothing else. I was so outdone at the way he was talking to me. No man had ever called me that word before. I wanted to cry but I remembered that there was nowhere in this house with these people in which I could be by myself. I withdrew from him after that. He didn't have to worry about me saying anything or asking for anything ever again. I wasn't doing a lot of talking to anyone after that. I had to witness him giving stuff to another young lady that lived in the house. He joked with her and then after a few days he would call her out her name to. She took it in stride. At least that's what it looked like. I wasn't used to being spoken to like that. I couldn't take it in stride. I looked around and noticed that he spoke to his own sisters like that if he felt like it. And then they would argue. He would laugh like it was cute and leave the room. Why does he talk to women like this? It's not nice. I started to not like him anymore. I no longer liked him as a person. I came outside on a Saturday and was just going to hang out in the driveway like everybody else. He turned to me cussed me out so bad in front of everyone that was outside. I tried to ignore him until everyone was looking at me. I just went back in the house. I didn't say anything to anyone. One night he came to get me out of my bed, I tried to play sleep. I knew he was standing there waiting for me to move, but I was hurt, embarrassed, and I didn't want to have anything else to do with him. But he just kept bumping my leg and telling me to come on.

Then I felt that maybe if I gave him what he wanted, he would stop treating me like this. So, I went with him. I didn't want to go. But he had manipulated my mind to think that I had to give him what he wanted in order for him to stop degrading me. I was feeling mentally and emotionally forced. He was quiet for a few days and then the degrading started again. And he would come and get me. And the degrading would happen all over again and again and even worse at times. The Good twin's baby momma tried to stand up for me one time. He told her to shut up b*itch before I slap you. He had big hands. I would not want him to ever slap me. So, I just tried to stay out of his way. But that didn't stop him from treating me like I was nothing. Like dirt at the bottom of his shoe. Everybody else was used to this type of behavior. I was torn up inside. I was afraid of him. And I had no one to talk to about any of this. I was scared to say anything to my aunt or his sister. I felt like they wouldn't believe me. I felt that they would insist that since I was 18 years old that I must have wanted it to happen. But I didn't. So, this secret I kept to myself. I was going to take it to my grave. I felt ashamed. And he made me feel even more ashamed every time he opened his mouth to me or about me. In between those times I met a young man that came to the house frequently.

I remember seeing him shortly after I moved there. It was a short thought because from the looks of it he was with one of my other Aunts. At least that's what it looked like. She was braiding his hair. He wore an afro. One day he came over and she wasn't there. He asked me if I knew how to braid, I was nervous because I knew that I wasn't that good of a braider. And I told him so. He didn't care. He just wanted his hair braided. I was nervous. Sweating under my arm pits. I braided his hair. He said Thank you. I said you're welcome.

He left. Later that evening a few of us were sitting outside and he came back with a couple of other young boys. We were talking about nothing in particular. Another guy who lived up the street was outside with us. He was actually trying to talk to me. I just laughed at him. I had already been warned about him. And told him so. The young man whose hair I braided, and the guy from up the street, and myself were across the street from the house talking. The guy from up the street told us he would be back. By the time he came back this guy and I were in the back seat of the car that belonged to the guy from up the street. One thing led to another and that's that. I tried to hold back any thoughts of liking him besides thinking he was a cool dude. I would have liked to hang out with him from time to time. I needed an escape from this house and from him, the evil twin. I start noticing that certain clothes were starting to feel tighter. I thought that maybe I had just gained weight from being over here with these people. They ate a lot. I thought that maybe I was eating a lot because I was depressed. I hang out with the "friend" and she's actually wondering if she was pregnant again by her husband. We both stole tests from a drug store. We took the tests in the store. I was pregnant. I could not believe this. I tell the niece that I'm friends with and we immediately think it's either the older guy or Mr. Tall, Dark and mysterious. In other words, I had to have been pregnant when I moved there. It seemed like the word spread extremely fast. All of a sudden everybody knew I was pregnant. And all assumed the same thing. That it had to have happened before I moved there. Everyone was saying this. So, I assumed they were right. I still considered the guy with the afro a possibility. Deep inside I asked myself if

Evil twin was a possibility. I immediately rejected it.

And refused to ever entertain the thought ever again. Not the way he was still talking to me. He would deny it anyway. I'd be a liar. And I was not prepared to handle the uproar that would come with that while I was still staying in this house with these people. No way. I could better deal with the rejection from the others. But his rejection always came with something evil. I lost my job for not wearing business casual every day except Fridays. I didn't know what I was going to do. Hanging out with "friend" and she's suggesting an abortion in so many words. Well it's not considered murder if you do it by this certain time. That was never an option for me. I am in a place I don't belong. I have no job. No other place to go. How am I going to take care of my baby? "Friend" and I went to apply for Medicaid, Food Stamps, and TANF. She explained to me that the TANF was money that I would get once a month for my child. Or children now. She would come get me with the excuse of needing my help cleaning up her house. My Aunt would talk bad about me in front of "Friend" "She won't do anything here. What she going do at your house?" I was always feeling embarrassed by this family. At least by certain ones. Remember I'm still a foreigner in a land that is not of my own. And I felt that every minute. My pregnancy was progressing. I was going to the doctor. My parents came and got my daughter. So, I was all alone. The Good twin was now out of the house and he and his kids were in an apartment of their own. It had gotten broken into. The mom was gone again so everyone thinks she had something to do with it. My Aunt volunteers me to house sit during the day while he was at work, since I wasn't doing anything except sitting around the house. Never asked me if I minded. I didn't but give me the choice.

This part of the family was like bullies to us outsiders. I often wondered what made the children's mother just decide take off so much and just leave everything. Kids, clothes, everything. I'm wondering if she was ever feeling what I was feeling from certain one's in this family. I'm wondering if the twins acted exactly alike. I decided that I didn't want to find out. He comes to get me that evening from the house. He tells me that he needs help straightening up his apartment. We get there, walk in the door and absolutely nothing is out of place. The apartment was spick and span. Not even a dirty dish in the sink. I'm like What's up? I went to the kitchen to get something to drink and he walks up behind me and just sniffs my neck. I'm so afraid right now. He tells me to make myself comfortable while he put his children to bed. So, I have a seat in a chair in the living room. My heart is about to jump out of my chest as he walks back into the room. He was a gentle man. My whole body felt like it was on fire. I couldn't cool down. He got down on his knees in front of me and started telling me how beautiful I was and that I deserved more. I deserved better. I was so much better than the things I was doing. I was stunned. I didn't know what to think of this. Was this going to be like what it was with the Evil twin? I was frozen in the chair. I wanted to disappear. I wanted to be anywhere except that house and where I was all together. He was still talking. He wants to make love to me. What? Then I started feeling ashamed already. Is that what I am? Everything the Evil twin says I am? Does the Good twin know what happened? They're twins. Maybe they share everything. Why me? What have I gotten myself into? Well there's no other way out of this. I was mentally surrendering. I couldn't fight him. I tried to stand up, but he was kissing me. He wrapped his arms around me.

He was whispering in my ear about the first time he saw me and was stuck when I smiled and said Good Morning. I was so tired of being noticed at this point. I wanted to ask him if his brother had told him anything. Too scared. I was so quiet. He told me he was going to make me scream. He wanted to give me pleasure that I've never had. In other words. He tried but I was afraid to say anything. After what should have been a beautiful night compared to others that I had, we went to sleep holding each other. I hadn't realized what I was doing until I felt his baby son climbing between us. I was too done then. Reality check. He's not mine either. I will forever belong to no one. After I went back home his attitude stayed true to his feelings. He would come in to get his kids and ask me if I was going home with him. I would shake my head no. He would loudly tell his mom that he was taking me home to help him clean up. I'm like you liar. He would pull me in a dark room and steal kisses from me. In another room at another time he would look right into my eyes while he touched me and wanted a reaction, but I never gave him one. He would always say he was going to make me scream. I never did. I'm about 4 or 5 months pregnant now, and I decide to go visit my dad in Minnesota for my birthday. I needed to get away. Too many secrets, too much depression. I was feeling suffocated in this house. The Good twin took me to do my laundry and to the bus station. I was to call him when I came back, and he would come and get me. The whole ride on the bus was numbing. I wanted to be excited about seeing my dad for the first time since moving to Texas, but I was too stuck on the way my world has turned upside down in a matter of months. Or to be honest in the few short years of leaving my dad's house in 1989. Everything was ok with my pregnancy so far, oh except for the STD I had. I was taking medication for that. I made it to Minneapolis and wasn't even aware of my Dad walking up to me.

My mind was in shambles. I looked like I was going through something.
I wondered if my dad would notice. Faking was never anything I was good at. We got back to the house and talked about my bus ride. And the pregnancy. I was feeling ashamed about being at my dad's house, pregnant, and not married. Not even in a relationship to speak of. My dad was a minister. I felt like I was bringing shame to our family. I was there for a week. One day during the week, my dad and I were upstairs and he was ironing. I just started crying. He asked me was it that bad? I started crying even harder. I wanted him to tell me to come home. But it was evident that this was no longer my home. I felt even worse. I was missing my daughter at night, I called her once while I was gone. I talked to my childhood friends about possibly moving back to Minneapolis and staying with her family. To this day I'm glad I declined on that offer. The couple later got divorced. He was abusive. At the young age that I was, I was smart enough to know that

I did not want to be in the middle of that situation. I prayed at night before I went to bed and tried to read a Bible. I couldn't shake the dread of having to go back to this house and these people and especially him. I never wanted to come back. But my daughter was still in Texas. I would have needed to come back and get her. I was also worried that my mom and step-dad were turning my daughter away from me. It was the end of my trip. My dad took me back to the bus station. I started to get on the bus and felt a hand on my shoulder. I looked back and my dad was hugging me really tight. He told me he loved me, and I started to cry. I missed my daddy so much. I missed being his little girl. I missed hearing my dad preaching. I missed everything I grew up learning. I hated my present predicament. I hated me. It was all my fault.

If I had just done whatever my mom said I would still be at home. I was angry at myself. I frowned the whole pregnancy. I didn't want to be there. I came back and went to the doctor to find out that I was threatening a miscarriage and I was ordered to bed rest. I literally stayed in the bed all day. I wanted to disappear. I would get drug off the couch by the baby son mechanic till I just chased him all the way up the street. They would pick and pick at me. More embarrassment. I was tired of it. I went to my uncle's house for a weekend and went to church with them. But I still felt empty leaving. The same way I felt going in. No change at all. I'm about 8 months pregnant and my parents want me to come home and have my baby. I say ok.

Season 11

From Darkness to Light?

I came back home. I was still 8 months and big as a house. One Sunday morning I'm about to iron some clothes for church and my mom was sitting on the couch with her Bible and devotional. I'm ironing, and she starts talking about how something isn't settling about me being back. I mentally role my eyes because she's always like this. Why did they ask me to come back? Just to put me out again? I could have stayed in the darkness. Basically, my mom didn't want to go to church with me being pregnant with my second child and no husband. I was getting so big I couldn't fit anything. Not even shoes. So, I just stayed home. When my parents got home from church, they asked me if I had read any Word that morning while they were gone. I sure did. If for no other reason than that I knew they would ask. They asked me what I read. I told them, and they called me a liar. How can you ask me, and I answer and I'm a liar? You don't even know, you weren't here. I wasn't lying. But you don't argue with your self-righteous parents. Hypocrites. They're so above ever making mistakes. Life changing mistakes. Mom you had two kids out of wedlock before marrying my dad. All of a sudden, you're so Holy? I suddenly remember about how I didn't want to come back.

But I felt it must be better than where I was. But my mom did some degrading on a self-righteous level. Hell at least the Evil twin was honest and consistent about his evilness. This fake stuff here puts a thorn in my butt.

You walk around the apartment and see scriptures all over the place. But can't see any evidence of the scriptures in their lives. I tried my best to just stay out of their way. They called themselves sitting me down like they did my sister about her second pregnancy. Oh, I see what this is. Well my situation was nothing like my sister's. So, I was unmoved by their little talk. My daughter was once again in a daycare. I was happy about that. But I wasn't happy about my mom treating me like a babysitter and not my daughter's mom. She's giving me instructions on how to take care of her while they go out and stuff like that. One day my daughter had a mosquito bite on her butt. She had scratched it until it became a scar. Well my mom comes in and gets ready to give her a bath, sees the scar and immediately accused me of putting the scar there from a spanking. The way my mom was handling me about my daughter made me scared to do anything. I didn't even want to comb her hair. It was ridiculous. And then you're accusing me of something I didn't do. I grabbed my stuff and went outside. My stepdad was outside with my uncle. I was standing by the car waiting for them to finish talking and I was going to ask my Uncle to take me back to the darkness. I didn't come here for this. If she (my mom) didn't really want me here, why did she ask me to come home?! It was no longer my home. If it ever was in the first place. I was so upset. I'm exhausted. My step-dad asked me what happened, and I told him. He told me to come back upstairs. I was so done with her I just wanted to leave. He told me it was late. Sleep on it. I couldn't sleep. I knew my mom.

She would wake you up early in the dark morning just to have an argument with you. And then you were supposed to be able to go back to sleep? Crazy. Time for the baby to arrive. Another girl. 8 lbs. 12 oz. Beautiful baby girl. Both my daughters were beautiful. No post-partum depression with this one. I was already depressed.

My mom didn't really want to deal with the new baby. That was fine. I was determined that I wasn't going to let her get near her and ruin her like she did my first daughter. Christmas is a few days away now and my parents were into it. I try to stay out of the way. My mom asks me to go to the car and see if I can find something in

the trunk. I couldn't find what she was talking about. She asked me if I saw everything in the trunk? I was dumbfounded. Of course, I saw everything in the trunk. You had me looking for something in the trunk. What kind of question was that? She gets mad. I said look I don't know what your problem is, but I was in my room minding my own business. If you didn't want me to see what was out there why did you send me out there? So then, she starts trying to talk to me about whatever the problem was between her and my step-dad. I tried to stay out of that. She got mad because I wasn't going to take any body's side. She tried to put me out then. You're going to put me out because I won't take sides? It's not my business. Keep it in your room. She told me to get out. I called my sister and she took me back to the darkness. About an hour later my step-dad came and got me and took me back to the house. I let my baby stay with the niece I was friends with. My step-dad was going to bring me to get her this weekend. I had made a decision right then that I was going to talk to the niece about letting my baby stay with her until
I could get her back. My mom tripped too much and was always telling me to get out.

I wanted to make sure that whenever she put me out again, because I was convinced it would happen again, I didn't want to worry about not having a place to stay with my baby. My oldest daughter went everywhere with me.
I can handle being out with her but not with a brand-new baby.

So, my baby girl was in the darkness. Funny though, my mom's attitude was better after I sent the baby away. Time went on and I was missing my daughters. Both of them. Even though one was with me every day. At least physically. A lady at church was a Supervisor at a hospital in the Housekeeping Department. She let my step-dad know that they were hiring. I went and applied and got the job. I went to work every day I was scheduled. I started off riding with my supervisor, then sometimes my step-dad took me or I caught the bus. My step-dad picked me up at night. When it was time to get paid, I already intended to give something to my cousin for having my baby. But I couldn't tell my mom that. She made sure I paid my tithes, paid her for taking my daughter to and from daycare and spend the rest of it on her. My oldest daughter. On my off days I would try to go see my baby. My mom would tell me "Fine, you can go as long as you're back before your other daughter is home from daycare". I was sad. By the time I got on the other side of town on the bus I would have to turn around and come back. I was angry and sad. I have another child on the other side of town that my mom won't let me see. That wasn't right. How did she feel when my dad stopped her from seeing us? Oh, she moved to another state and didn't even say good bye. That's what she did. I didn't want to be like that. So, one check I was able to give my cousin something. I had her come to my job and get it. She brought my baby girl. I hadn't seen her since she was about a month old. She was looking like me.

Frowning. I didn't know what to do. I started trying to get her on the weekends I was off. My mom always had a problem with this innocent baby being here. Was she jealous? I have two daughters. Nobody was going to get more than the other unless it was needed. My oldest daughter loved having a baby sister. She would go get her out of the bed and carry her all the way in to the living room. One day my step- dad and I went to the grocery store. When we came back, I heard my baby crying all the way from the parking lot. I ran up the stairs. I busted through the door. "What are you doing to her?!" She just won't stop crying. Yeah, she can tell that you don't like her. I was so hurt. I had to stop getting my baby. I'm thinking, "I know they think I just don't want her but that's not the situation." "They don't want me to be her mother right now." My baby is not going to know me because this b*tch of a mom I have won't let me see her or have her. I talked to my cousin constantly to let her know the situation. Meekeeyah why did you even go back over there knowing how your mom is? She said. I honestly don't know. A few months go by without me seeing my daughter. I miss her so much. But this lady won't let me have no time to miss anything. Everything was always about my oldest daughter. And it was always a competition of who my daughter would love the most. My mom has always wanted my daughter to herself. That threat stayed in the back of my mind. I was so tired of feeling unwanted, and unloved. I decided that I was going to end my life. I hated to leave my daughters but at the rate I was going I wasn't going to be able to be a mother to either one of them the way I wanted to. The next day on my way to work I decided to step off the curb in front of the next bus or 18-wheeler. I wanted something quick and instant. Here comes an 18-wheeler. I got ready to step off of the curb and I felt this hand on my shoulder pull me back. I started crying. I wanted to end this agony I was feeling in my heart.

I had lost all joy and happiness since moving to this retched city. If I ever had it at all. I went on to work. I never really just felt totally at ease with my step-dad. I never understood why. One night when he came to get me from work, we would sit in the living room and watch N.Y. Undercover and then go to bed. He would always want me to sit in his lap. The more he wanted me to sit in his lap, the more I felt uncomfortable.

After a couple of times of sitting in his lap, I started locking my bedroom door after going into my room. I would just have this uneasy feeling in the pit of my stomach. And good thing I moved with the feeling. A couple of times I heard him trying to turn the knob. This happened more than once. Another night after getting home, he grabbed me by my wrists and laughed an evil laugh while I struggled to break free. Then he shoved me back on the couch, letting go of my wrists. Then walked off laughing. What an evil face he had. I hurried to my room and locked the door. I was thinking, what is going on here. I was crying. After that he told me that he wasn't going to pick me up from work anymore. I didn't understand why. Nor did I ask. I called my older brother to come get me. I told him what happened and he told me to call him back in a few minutes. When I called him back, he lets me know that my mom was coming to get me. When she got there, she asked me why I didn't ask her? I thought that she was in agreement with my step-dad. She said that before she came to pick me up, she asked him why he made that decision. He said that it was because I never offered him any gas money. That next check I made sure to give him some money and he was back to picking me up. 90 days had pasted on the job and I was getting a raise. I was so excited. Had a conversation with my sister and she asked me about being a roommate with her. I told her I had to think about it.

I was about to get a raise and I needed to see what my money was going to look like. During this time, my mom had scheduled me to go to a resume class. She was refining my step-dad's resume. She was on a kick to have all of us making more money on jobs we really didn't want. My step-dad liked his job. And I guess I liked mine. I ran into an old friend of mine from church. She had a baby at the hospital I was working at. When she got home, we talked about me coming to stay with her and her family for a little while. I was going to leave my oldest my daughter with my mom until I got somethings settled. I had made up my mind that it was going to be that next Friday. I was off, but no one knew that. I was going to leave before anyone got home. I made a mistake telling my sister and she told on me. She was mad because I didn't want to be her roommate. I have never wanted to live with my sister. I didn't like the way she paid bills. So, my parents confronted me the day before I was going to leave. They tell me everything I told my sister as if they were on the phone with us.

And also, they let me know that my sister was mad because I didn't want to be her roommate. So Childish. They put me out again. On my way back to the darkness.

Season 12
Out of the pan and into the Fire

Luke 11:24-26 When the unclean spirit is gone out of a man, he walketh through dry places, seeking rest; and finding none, he saith, I will return unto my house whence I came out. And when he cometh, he findeth it swept and garnished. Then goeth he, and taketh to him seven other spirits more wicked than himself; and they enter in, and dwell there: and the last state of that man is worse than the first.

After some other detours, staying with the "friend" and her family, I ended up back in the darkness. And almost comfortable. When I say comfortable, I already knew what to expect. Nothing had changed since I left to have my baby. Or since sending my baby girl here.

This scripture above is referring to what happened when I went back to live with my parents and when I moved back to the darkness. When I went back home, I was in church regularly. Every Sunday I was there. That is where the cleaning out the house comes in. But because I had no one showing me how to really replace or fill the house up so that there was no room for anything else, I would leave church feeling empty. My house was empty. So, it was all too familiar and comfortable to get back to the darkness and have those spirits move right back in. But they brought guests. They threw a party. Watch this.

I came back to the darkness and the feelings of hurt, betrayal, shame, and everything else was there constantly reminding me of the events that happened when I first moved there. But I was resolved to the fact that that's the way things were, so I got used to the depression. The "friend" and I were still hanging out every once in a while. My aunt tells me one day, "You're either going to die or get locked up behind that girl". I paid no attention to it. One day the "friend" calls me and says we were going to lunch with this guy. She picks me up. Any other day my oldest daughter would ask me if she could go and I would tell her no. This day, she never asked. We go get the guy, and then go to Wal-Mart. When we get there, she hands me some money. She tells me a list of things to get first and what the cashier looked like that I needed to deal with. And whatever amount was left, I could get whatever I wanted. So I do everything she said. I make it to the register and don't have enough money. I leave the line to go back out to the car for more money. I hear a voice so clear say, "Stay in this car", I disregarded it and went back into the store. I couldn't find the money and I just took some things out of the basket. I'm leaving the line and a police officer is walking beside me. I'm asking him if I needed an escort to my car. Stupid.

He politely let's me know that I was being arrested. Arrested? For what? They put me in the car and I remember the voice. Why didn't I just listen? I go to jail and I'm booked in for Theft by Counterfeit. The next day, I'm called out to go talk to Secret Services. I was crying . I didn't know anything. Honest. They let me know that I wasn't the one they were after. They want the person printing the money. I didn't have that information. But I gave them all that I knew about the girl I was with and the guy. I didn't care. She wasn't my friend. She got away and I'm in jail. The next day I'm being released. Someone bonded me out. I'm scrounging for money to take the bus home. "Friend" comes to see me early the next morning. She thinks she scaring me about telling me what that guy was capable of doing if he got in trouble. That's your friend. Not mine. Why should I care? He bonded you out. She says. With counterfeit money. I just shake my head. Unbelievable. A little more conversation and she leaves. I don't see her again for some years. One particular evening when Evil twin was being his normal self. He was again talking bad to me and I was just sitting on the couch trying to ignore him. He went on and on. This time his baby sister, who I was tight with. And who had my baby, took up for me. "Why are you always messing with her? Just leave her alone". Their arguing went on for a while. He got up from the table that was positioned behind me. He walked by me and back hands me in my nose with his fist. I saw stars. I was stunned. He hit me so hard that my nose should have bled but didn't. Not a drop. His younger nieces were afraid for me and tried to put me in their bedroom in case he decided to come back. At that point I was feeling like "What else could he possibly do to me?" The damage was done. I thought. That was just the icing on the cake. His sister, the one that took up for me, had gotten on Section 8 housing and was getting ready to move in a house across the street. She said I could move in with her. I did.

And was starting to feel a little at ease because he wasn't over there that much. At first.

I began to gain weight from just sitting around. Some guy friends that I used to go to school with show up one day to see me. One was the young man that rejected me before my sophomore year in high school, and the other one used to like my sister. I was glad to see them. It had been a long time. We caught up on some old times and they left. A couple of days later just one of the guys comes back. He was a very good friend of mine. I didn't think anything of it. He mentioned that he wanted to talk to me about something but kept putting it off for some reason. We would chit chat on the phone at night, but he still never said what he wanted to talk about. About two weeks of this and then we finally start to talk about something. He asks me to open a bank account at a very prestigious bank for him. He said he couldn't for some reason. I was not thinking anything about it.

The next day we go and open this account. No more talk for another few days or so. I'm depressed because I have no money and can't take care of my daughters. My friend comes to me and asks me if I wanted to make some quick money. He assures me that the plan is flawless and that I won't get caught. I was still stuck on quick and money. I said yes. What do I have to do? He gives me some details and tells me he will let me know when we are to ride out. I talk to my cousin about this because if I ended up going to jail, I wanted to make sure that my daughters could stay with her. She said ok. The next Wednesday was when it was going down.

He came and got me, and we were gone most of the day. I

came back home and the whole block knew where I had gone and had their hands out. Well We're keeping this a secret for you. For a small fee. The only person I felt I owed anything to would be my cousin because she had my girls. But remember the bullies. I found me a job shortly after that. But right before

I started the job, FBI show up at my cousin's house. They want to talk to me about the adventure I had with my friend not even a week ago. They let me know that I will be indicted and will have to go to court. The bank was pressing charges for Conspiracy. They said that I would be getting a phone call or something in the mail letting me know when I had to go to court. In the meantime, some trouble had started between some guys and the block was getting shot up almost every day. One of the guys involved was a friend of my guy friend. The one I got in trouble with. I called him to talk to him about his dealings with the situation. He let me know that the guy was his friend. I reminded him that me and my children are over here. . If he couldn't leave the situation alone, I wasn't going to able to be his friend anymore. I was concerned about my children's safety. And as my friend I felt like he should have been to. But that was not the case. We were no longer friends. The school year began and my daughter was going to school. Everything was good until I get a call from my mom. She tells me to tell my daughter good bye for her because she was moving back to Minnesota for good. I was pissed off. Tell her yourself. So she went and had lunch at the school with my daughter and left. Yeah don't do her like you did me and my brother. Have guts enough to say good bye. My daughter started getting in trouble at school just about every day. I would get a call from the school. I would walk to go get her. Bring her home to punish her and then take her back. It happened almost every day.

I didn't know what to do. I called my old pastor's wife and asked her to pray with me about my daughter's behavior. She did. But it didn't get better for a while. I was out of options.

I eventually got a court date. I called the detectives to let them know that I didn't have a way to get to Dallas. They came to pick me up.

They had to handcuff me. I was hoping my daughters were still asleep so they would not have to see this. This was talked about for days. After that, I started the new job. I worked there until right before Christmas. I got fired. I was depressed because I wasn't going to be able to get my kids anything for Christmas. I was fired for stealing time. Being on the clock and wasn't working.

I had to go renew my ID, so as I was leaving to go catch the bus, this old, old guy who was obviously an acquaintance of the family asks me if I needed a ride. I said no thank you I was going to catch the bus. He insisted on helping me save my bus fare for another day. So, I said ok. I got into the truck with him and he drives off. While we're driving, he asks me if he could perform oral sex on me and he would give me $50. I was so ashamed of myself before I even gave him an answer because I'm sitting in this seat thinking "I need this money". I said ok. We went to a motel room and I let him do what he wanted. He gave me the money and we got back in the truck and he took me to the DMV. He told me that he would wait for me and take me back home. I said ok. But after I did what I needed to do concerning my ID, I snuck out another door and ran. I felt filthy, dirty, slimy, empty. Ashamed. I was becoming very familiar with this feeling of being shamed. I was ashamed of myself. Have I come to such a low as this right here?

I remember talking to my sister and she was letting me know about some lows that she experienced and how she got through it. I was not comforted by her story. I still felt like the dirt I was walking on. I knew better. I really didn't know how I knew better but I did. And I was ashamed of myself. I determined that I was never doing that again. During this winter season, my step-dad starts having seizures. We went to see him in the hospital. I was scared and cried and cried. I had never wanted to see him like that. My uncle said that they were at work having a conversation in the office and he just went into a seizure. He was finally able to come home from the hospital, but he now lived alone. The family volunteers me to go stay with him for a while. I had to set up his doctor appointments.

Make sure he was taking his medication on time. These episodes made him digress in his mind. Back to when he was younger. Funny thing was that he didn't forget about me. He would ask for me at the hospital.

While I was staying there, my mom calls. She says Thank you to me for being there to take care of him. Well you're not. So who else was going to do it? My sister stayed in the apartments right across the street and never came to see him. Unless she needed something of course. I was disgusted to have been related to either one of them. My step-dad was feeling so much better and he decided that he didn't need me there anymore. So I went home and I then had another job at a call center. I went to apply and had to take a typing test. I failed it, but I knew the HR person and she put me through any way. I was grateful. I liked my job. I was there every day at the most. Until I had to change to a later shift and it began to be hard for me to get home. I was blessed to have rides with my co-workers, but something would happen, and they would be gone.

Then I had to find someone else or pay someone from the house gas money to come get me from the other side of town. I ran into a guy who used to be a neighbor when I was in middle school.

He lets me know how he had always felt about me, and we started meeting up in the bathroom to mess around. It was my weekly escape before going home and dealing with the darkness. Some people cope by using a substance, I coped with sex. I later realized that I had addict behavior. Going forward I ended up losing the job. I lost the job because I had to go to Dallas for court. The Fed agents came and got me from the house. They told me that everything would go well, and I would be back home that evening. So, I had to go sit in the Federal Jail until court time. I was up next. When I stood before the judge, told me my charges and decided that since I wasn't a flight risk, meaning I wasn't going to give the courts a hard time when it was time to go to court, he was going to let me go home on my own recognizance. But I had a warrant in my county and I had to stay in Dallas jail. I wasn't going home.

I was just determined to get through this. I had been in jail before. I could handle it. I was not afraid. I was gone for a few days. Then I hear my name being called. They told me to get my stuff, I was being released. I was surprised because I wasn't aware that my people knew the outcome of that court appearance. I was wrong. I walked outside and my aunt, both her daughters and my baby girl came and got me from the Dallas County jail. I was happy to see them. They let me know that the Good twin had put up the money to get me out and that I needed to make sure that I paid him back. I did that to. I immediately paid him back that next pay check. Going to court was not over though. That is why I lost my job. I was gone for those days and didn't call in. Back at square one again.

I need another job. A friend of mine told me about her job but I didn't get it. I ended up doing little assignments through staffing places but nothing permanent. Just to try to keep some money flowing in. During all of this, remember I stated earlier that my mom had left for good right? Well she comes back to visit my step-dad that summer.

She and I had had some words regarding my daughters while she was here. She wanted one and not both. She did for one and not both. She wanted to take my oldest daughter to the doctor for basically something that was not an emergency and I wouldn't give her my daughter's Medicaid card. Then she left, back to Minnesota. One day I was out with one of my younger cousins doing some job hunting. I filled out an application at this warehouse. They were hiring through one of the staffing places that I worked through. We were on our way back to the house and my pager goes off. I call my cousin because it was a 911. She lets me know that Child Protective Services was there looking for me and that they would be back. We got to the house and I was really trying to rack my brain to figure out who would have done this. My cousin says, "You know who did this". I call my mom and ask her if she made that call.

She told me to ask them. That was all I needed to hear. I went so cold in that moment. I told her "You are messing with the wrong b*tch". And I had to hang up. I was beyond furious. The picking just won't stop. The tantrum was because she didn't get her way. I had to call my Daddy. I told him "You will not believe what your ex-wife just did to me". I told him. He tried his best to calm me down. He wouldn't get off the phone until I was calm. The next day the investigator came. He was a nice man.

He asked his questions, looked around the home, looked at my daughters. He let me know that the investigation was closing in the next 30 days. We explained to him about my mom. He understood and let me know I had nothing to worry about. That was a relief. Or so I thought. I could not believe that she would stoop so low. Everything that she had already done to me wasn't enough? Why did she keep messing with me? And she was acting like a coward making the call and then going back out of the state. I was beyond furious. Even more so because I couldn't get to her. I had to go to court one more time on this Federal case. I can't remember how I got there. I was sentenced to 5 years of probation with restitution.

I was so relived. I had a great attorney, court appointed. He explained to me the ruling system for Federal cases. The Evil twin tried to scare me into thinking that I was going directly to prison. Nope. Not yet anyway. I had gotten the job at the warehouse right after going to court. I didn't have to start reporting for another month. I started working and was feeling a little better. I had a way to work until I started getting paid and then I was riding the bus. Now there was a guy that I had been seeing off and on for a little over a year. He was nice to me. That was pretty much it. He would come get me for some weekend and we just hung out in a room, at somebody's house. Not a motel. I began to get upset about somethings he would do that I felt were disrespectful. But because we weren't exactly a couple, I felt that I had no reason to get upset. But that didn't stop me. I rode the bus every day to work. Pretty much the same people rode this bus to. There was a girl about my age and we worked together. She was cool, and we would talk or fall asleep on the bus. For the most part she was quiet. She had let me know that she was getting a car soon. I was genuinely happy for her.

She was excited to. It was her very first car. She was tired of driving her mom's. She had gotten her car. I asked her if she could take me to report on the day I needed to go, but she told me that she couldn't. I let her know that I would give her gas money. She had said she couldn't help me. Well that put me in a dilemma because I was going to have to miss work that day if I couldn't find somebody to take me. I had to go to my manager and let him know the situation. He told me to try harder about finding help with that. I couldn't think of any one at that moment. I tried for two days to find someone but to no avail. The next day I went to work, was my last.

I was let go because it was very important to be at work and I was still in my probation period. I was back at square one again. I eventually did find someone to take me. At least drop me off and I figured out a way home. The friend from work showed up at my house one day. She wanted me to ride with her. I was happy to see her. I just thought when I left the job, we would lose contact. She was telling me how her and her sister had moved into a new apartment. She asked me if I had ever made it to the appointment I had. I told her I did. And was out in time to still had made it to work. She asked me why I didn't ask her again.

I thought what a strange question. Why would I ask again after you already said no., I don't do that? She offered to take me the next time. I said ok. I asked her how she was doing and everything, she said good. Work was good. We talked about some people from the job. And then she took me home.

She said she was nervous about coming to see me. I asked her why? She really didn't have an answer. The next weekend she came and got me again and we had to stop at her apartment for something. I was just going to wait in the car, but she told me to come up and meet her sister. I was like ok. I stepped into the door and just stayed where I was. I didn't go any further into the apartment. I wasn't staying long. I thought. I met her sister. They were identical twins like

Evil and Good. They had children. She had two daughters and her sister had a son and a daughter. Going forward I'll be referring to them as Sick and Twisted. WE hung out a little more after that day and I approached her with the idea of me and my children moving in with them. All of our kids were around the same age. She told me that she would talk it over with her sister and get back to me.

In the meantime, Evil was making ugly comments about Sick. How she looked like a butch, and how she was riding me around like I was her girlfriend. At my cousin's house we always went to sleep with the television on. I slept in the living room. I would wake up and see porn movies on. I would fall asleep with thoughts in my head. And in my spirit. Sick had gotten back with me and she said her sister was good with it and to wait a week or so. I was ok with that because I was seeing the light out of this darkness. At least that is what I thought. A few days before my children and I left, I had a dream that my cousin and I got into it, I left but I came back. I would wake up in the middle of the night praying in tongues. The night before I was to leave, my cousin and I had an argument.

My children and I left. We stayed gone the weekend. I talked the situation over with the sisters. They let me know where I was wrong and that I needed to apologize to my cousin.

That Monday morning, I came home and apologized, and we stayed. The next week I had a dream that my cousin and I had another argument, my daughters and I left, and didn't come back that time. Again, I woke up in the middle of the night praying in tongues. The argument happened. I wasn't wrong this time. I called Sick and asked her to come early in the morning and get us. We were not coming back. She said ok right after I pick my sister up from work. Late that night I started putting our stuff in the garage, so I could get it out in the morning. I washed our clothes and bagged up everything and moved it in front of the garage door. When I heard the knock on the door the next morning, I lifted the garage and had Sick put our stuff in the car, and I grabbed my girls. We were out of there. I couldn't breathe until we were on the freeway heading to their apartment. And then I was still scared to breathe. I thought I was dreaming. I was gone. I had both of my babies. No one was left behind anywhere.

I was 22 years old. My daughters were almost 5 and almost 2. When we got to the apartment, unloaded everything, we were finally able to sit down in some peace. I hadn't felt peace in a very long time. I wanted to cry from pure bliss, but I was afraid that the sisters would think I was crazy. So, I just kept myself together and tried to process the fact that I just might be in a better place. The sisters asked me what I wanted to do while I was there and that they were willing to help me. Well, I had always wanted to have a medical degree. My step-dad had started having seizures right after my mom left him. So, I wanted to be able to take care of him if I ever needed to.

There was a Vocational College not far from their apartment, that had a course for Medical

Assistant. We looked into it. I was surprised that they wanted to help me. They acted like it was the normal thing to do. They both worked. Twisted worked over nights at a hospital, and Sick worked at the warehouse that I was working at during the day. The children seemed to be getting along. No one was making fun of anybody. No crying. No one was in any danger. And we went to church. I was so relieved about that. I couldn't wait to get back to church. I felt like I was starving for something. That first Sunday we all went, I felt like God was talking directly to me. I cried practically the whole service. I left church feeling relieved. God was still with me. Everything seemed to be going well. I woke up the next morning feeling Sick pulling on my leg. She was trying to wake me up. I was so tired. I
got up and the sisters were talking and laughing about stuff. I was feeling weird about something. Something was different, I just didn't know what. So, the next night when Twisted was at work, Sick and I were on her bed talking and then we were both laying on our backs looking at the ceiling. I guess I had dosed off because then I felt her rubbing on my thigh and then she was on top of me.

She must have been just as shocked as I was, because she hurried up and got off of me. She was feeling really shy. I just sat up and tried to process what just happened. I had never experienced this before and wasn't sure what to say about it. We started talking about somethings that we were feeling and stuff that was on television late at night. The Porn movies. She let me know that she was realizing that she might have feelings for me when I was still at my cousin's house and she thought I could read her mind. That's why she was nervous about coming to see me. I understood that.

She also let me know the things that Twisted had said about her hanging out with me. They were exactly the same things that Evil had said. That Sick was riding me around like I was her girlfriend. I didn't think too much about it when Evil said it because that was just him, Evil. I have had other female friends that I rode around with and things like this were never said. What was the difference here? I tried to figure it out. Only for a minute. Then I found myself having extreme feelings for this girl. She was helping me, she wanted to see me succeed. And she cared about me. I was hurting and vulnerable and fell right in. That's where those 7 more demons came in. Being around like spirits. She evidently had that spirit already and because I wasn't full in my spirit with the right stuff, God, Jesus, The Word, I was open to this spirit of Lesbianism. I wasn't afraid of showing how I felt about her. But Twisted was having a self- righteous moment and was trying to use scripture to point the finger at Sick's wrong. They don't know that I saw that. So now I'm in school and I have this girlfriend that all of a sudden doesn't want to be that anymore. I mean very quick. I was messed up. I didn't understand how a person can start something and then just cut it completely off. I was hurt. I was getting distracted at school and could no longer concentrate. She didn't want to be with me but at night she wanted me. I was confused.

She needed to make up her mind. I went to Twisted and tried to talk to her about what was going on. I was not looking for what was about to happen next. She sat there and listened to me, told me that I just needed to try to move on. And then I felt her hand on the back of my neck. I was looking at her and she was looking at me in a real dreamy like facial expression.

Next thing I know she's kissing me. And not like she was new to what was going on. She stopped and asked me if she did something wrong.

I was just dumbfounded by the whole thing. Everything was getting really weird. I'm in this house with both of these girls and they both want me. I told her that I thought she had a problem with me and Sick being together. She stated only because she wanted me to. That Sunday we were at church and all of a sudden Sick was getting paranoid. She said that the pastor was saying something about us being together, but I didn't hear that. Then she thought people were whispering about us. Well who knew about it? I hadn't told anyone. Believe me. And so, the triangle had started. I was being with Twisted during the day, and with Sick at night. Trying to keep things under wraps. I had gotten a call from the Good twin. He wanted to see me. He told me he was on his way. I asked Twisted if she minded watching my girls while I left with him. She said ok. I had opened up to them about a lot of things by now. He pulled up, I got into the car. He drives off. He tells me that he was missing me and lied to everyone about going to get ice cream, just so he could come see me. I didn't care what he told the people, I was happy to see him. I needed the escape from what was happening where I now lived. He took me to a motel room. We went in and he couldn't get my clothes off fast enough. I wish we could just be together, and nobody care he said. I think I told him I loved him. I did love him. And I could feel the way he felt about me. He would always tell his baby momma when she came home that he was going to find another girl.

And he would look right at me. I was nervous. I didn't want anyone getting a clue. She wasn't taking him seriously. It didn't matter. He already had another girl. Me. That high was over and he took me back home. I asked when I was going to see him again. He couldn't tell me. I was exhausted by the love making.

I went right to sleep on the couch. Sick came home and asked me if I was ok. I told her what happened and went back to sleep. I was really trying to hurt her because she was playing games with me. I couldn't tell her about me and Twisted. Twisted was always upset seeing me and Sick together, playing around, or just talking. I was going to hear about it the next morning after she got home from work. She went into her room and tried to take a nap before work. Sick told me to go and wake her up. I tried. She wouldn't get up. She sent me back. I pulled the covers off of her. We tussled over the blanket and then she kissed me really quick. Sick walked in and I hurried up and got out of the room. Look, you might be reading this book and looking at the picture on the back and thinking she had it like that? Two sets of twins. Guys and girls. But if you pay attention to the names, I gave them you would recognize how these spirits were on me and I didn't know. I didn't know that there was a battle going on for my soul. Every time the evil got too close to me the good would come and remind me of how I was supposed to be treated. I wasn't trying to be a player at all. Some of you have been through worse and more wiled out situations. Don't judge me. I'm determined to finish this book. The enemy wants me to be ashamed, but I am no longer ashamed of these so- called secret sins. Being ashamed means I'm still in bondage to this mess but I am not. Going forward, praise God.

I didn't know that I was never going to be with the Good twin like that ever again. He tripped over some cord in his garage and had a blood clot in his leg. I got a call from my aunt that I had mail at her house. I walked in and he was sitting in a chair.

He was looking so intently at me. I said hello. I thought that was why he was looking at me so hard. I was feeling uncomfortable. I looked at my mail in my hand, asked my aunt if that was all of it? She said yes. I looked at him one more time and I left. I was never going to see him again. The next week I got a call from the older sister that the blood clot had rose to his heart and exploded. She told me she was going to let me know about the wake and funeral. I didn't know what to think. I was never going to see him again. The only one who truly felt something real about me. He was just scared of the backlash from the family. I felt my heart breaking. I no longer cared about either one of these girls. I ended up quitting school. I had too much going on at home. I couldn't give it my best. The guy that I had been seeing off and on decides to show up. I was tired of the way he was treating me. He started to get undressed, I told him to stay right there I had to go get the kids from the bus stop. No, I didn't. Not for another hour, but I was sick of the kibbles and bits that he always handed me. I went out the door and hid out of sight. I was able to see him when he left. Good riddance. I went to the Good twin's wake feeling like everyone new about us. I had just recently found out that I was pregnant to. But I wasn't sure who it belonged to. The Good twin or the guy I had been seeing. Well since the Good twin was gone, I was going with the other guy. The funeral was unbearable for me. Especially when we got to the point of everyone walking up to view the body. It was an open casket funeral. I couldn't take any more.

I walked over to my aunt, gave her a hug, and let her know that I was not going to be able to go to the grave site. She said she understood and that was ok. Thank you for coming. I looked quickly at the evil twin and walked out of the church. Thank me for coming? Of course, I was coming. I loved him.

After the New Year, stuff started hitting the fan. Twisted started giving me ultimatums about telling Sick about us. What was I going to do? How was I going to tell her?

Did I care about her knowing? Of course, I cared. Right? I mean look at the games she kept playing with me. So, I told her that I needed to talk to her. We went to a park on the northside of town. She kept asking me what I wanted to talk about. She asked me if it was someone else. I just looked at her and found myself crying. I got out of the car.
I needed air. I couldn't tell her that me and her sister were sneaking around. But I knew I needed to tell her the truth. It was hard. We got

back in the car, we did our thing for what I meant to be the last time and we went back home. Twisted just looked at me. She could tell that I didn't tell her. It ended up coming out. Twisted had turned on me. She blurted it out. I was wide eyed. I was feeling a déjà vu. My sister. Sick asked me was she lying, I said yes. I looked her right in the eye and lied. She knew who was lying. She started throwing things at me. Every time she thought about it, she threw something at me. Twisted just sat there and watched. The very air was different after that. Twisted left to go stay with her mom and then came back. Now the twisted stories and exaggerations begin. All towards me. I came to their house with this spirit, I manipulated them in to thinking I had never done anything with girls before. The way I wore my clothes. My mind was really asking myself if these things are true? I was different from them.

We had the same exact birthday. They were two years older than me. Sick decides she wants me after all, if for no other reason than the fact that she didn't want Twisted to have me. They almost fought over me. I didn't want to be with either one of them. But I had nowhere else to go. Sick wanted to move out, so we went to stay at her friend's house. She had the same spirit. While staying at this house I started praying, a lot.

I wanted God to do whatever He needed to so that this could all end. Not knowing that it was just getting started. I prayed and prayed. Holding her hand, I was praying. I ended up having a miscarriage with the baby. I was lost about that. I didn't understand. But I was dealing with it. Their mom implied that it was because I was living in sin. Or the truth behind the father of this baby died so the baby was dying to. I didn't know. Sick was changing. She was becoming mean to my kids. She was picking on them a lot. Twisted was pregnant also. We all eventually ended up at this lady's house. I wanted Twisted dead for the betrayal. I was thinking about how I could have set that apartment on fire but got the kids out and not her. I even called my dad one day. I said, "Daddy, I'm thinking about doing really harmful to somebody". All he said was, "I know you'll do the right thing". End of conversation. Twisted lived another day. But I did do this. I was supposed to pick the kids up after school. Even Twisted's son. I went to the school and told them that his mom was coming to get him. And I left with the girls. I didn't call Twisted or anything. She eventually got a call from the school about picking him up. I felt a little better about what I did. But at the same time I felt bad because I've never done evil for evil. My heart wasn't feeling right at all about that. But I never mentioned it to anyone. Eventually Sick got an apartment of her own and we moved to the Eastside. She was still picking on my kids.

Twisted and her kids went back to stay with their mom. I was still being sent to go pick her up and take her to the doctor or run errands. Sick didn't want me talking to her but I was still being the taxi. The arguments increased. She would be ugly to my oldest when I was praising her about getting good grades. One morning Sick threw my daughter's money out the door. Another time I had left to go to the store and came back hearing my baby girl screaming at the top of her lungs. I ran as fast as I could. I bust through the door. What are you doing?! Déjà vu again. My mom. Sick wouldn't let go of her arm. It was a tug of war about my baby. Twisted just stayed out of the way. I put my body between Sick and my baby. She was so scared. No one would tell me what happened. To this day I still don't know what happened while I was gone. I immediately called my cousin. You have to come get her. I told her what happened. She was on her way. She came and got my baby. She was out of harm's way. Again. Sick was acting like my mom. My cousin told me that my daughter would be afraid of falling asleep because she thought Sick would come and get her. I was so sorry. I cried about the effects that my choices were having on my children. God what do I do? How can I get out of this? I'm praying for a way out. I had started a temp job and I had been driving Sick's car back and forth to work. One night she decides when I have 30 minutes to be at work that I couldn't take her car. I was hating her by now. She was still picking on my oldest daughter and I was trying to figure out a way to get her out.

The kids went to school. Twisted and I talked, and I encouraged her to get her own apartment. She went after one and got it. Now I had a way out for my other daughter. At least from Sick. Twisted was never mean to my girls. My problem with her was that she didn't fight enough for them because they were innocent. And I told her that. Twisted moved out. I was praying every day for the strength to move out and where to go. Sick had tried to choke me, she tried to force herself on me and I was just ready to go crazy. That Sunday I and my daughter walked down the street to the church. We were meeting Twisted and her kids. We get to the church and she starts telling me about a lady that started babysitting her kids. I asked her if she could have the babysitter come pick me up the next day so I could have a way to her house. She said that she would ask her.

My daughter was going home with Twisted. I had clothes and stuff. She was back to wanting to see me succeed. The service was so fresh and right on time. It gave me what I needed to be ok. I was leaving Monday before Sick came home from work. I moved in with Twisted and I got a job at an electronics company and got a car. I am feeling good. During this time the babysitter starts being mean to my daughter and I start taking her to my cousin's after she got out of school. Come to find out, Twisted had been talking about me behind my back to this lady. She told her that I had gotten a car and some other stuff. But the comments that were sporadically thrown about led me to believe that Twisted was being a backstabber. Twisted worked at another warehouse on the northside of town. When I got off work, I went to get my daughter and then her kids from the lady. Then I would go get her from work. If I hadn't have gotten the car, none of this would be happening. And she was talking about me behind my back.

Sick tried to come over and cause problems, but I didn't entertain. One day my batterie dies in my car and I have to get a new one. I had to wait for Twisted to bring me some money at the auto parts store. So I wait there. I met a man while waiting at the auto parts store. He eventually ended up being my next baby's dad. No doubt about it. I lost that job after 6 months. I found out I was pregnant. I applied for County Housing. During the summer I had another job working at the Housing Authority in HR. Through another Staffing service. I was finally approved for the housing and we moved to a city on the outskirts of Fort Worth. Twisted moved with me. She had gotten approved for County Housing, but she let Sick stay in her apartment. About a month away from me having my baby, my mom moves back to Fort Worth. She moves in with me. She started talking to the guy downstairs from us. I warn her that the man had a wife and she was just gone because they were fighting. That didn't stop her. She would take him to church. She went back to the church where the Pastors were helping me go to college. We went through some things and

I have my son. 8 lbs. 15 oz. Big boy. I was in love. My son. Shortly after having my son, Twisted and I have an argument and she moves out. My mom tells me to talk to God about whether to let her come back. I didn't know how to hear God at this time. I just went with my gut feeling. I let her come back. Sometime later, my lights get cut off. My mom was out and I call her to come home so that we can figure out how to get them back on. She comes home but does nothing to help. She was being unpleasant to Twisted. Along with some other things. I told her not to have that man up in my apartment when I wasn't there. We came home one night seeing through the window. My mom was calling herself quickly coming out the apartment. Not fast enough lady.

I end up telling my mom that if she wasn't going to help where she laid her head, then she had to go. Yes I was putting my mom out. I called my sister and she tells me about a lot of things that my mom was telling her behind my back about my kids and Twisted's kids. Oh no not staying in my house. My mom and I didn't talk again for a long time. I was applying for government assistance and needed a copy of my birth certificate. Well I knew my mom kept copies because we (her kids) were always losing them for whatever reason. I ask her for a copy and she tells me no. I call my step-dad and told him about the situation. Next thing I know, he tells me to go to her job the next day to get it.

I got another job at the closest nursing home. I was able to walk back and forth. It was literally right at the end of the block. There's this guy that I work with. He didn't talk to me at first. But then we were cool. He let me borrow his car a couple of times to take my babies to appointments and such. He takes me to lunch one day and quickly makes a decision that he was not wanting a relationship with me. Um, you didn't even give it a chance. Whatever. That was unexpected seeing as I didn't know he felt anything for me. I mean we kissed one time. But that says what?

I ended up leaving that job because the department changed managers and they let the newest person go. Me and the guy stayed in touch some. Then there were other jobs. That next Summer I was able to move in to a bigger apartment somewhere else due to the fact that I now have an additional child. I was now working at a mail sorting company in Arlington. So, I moved to another city on the outskirts of Fort Worth. In the opposite direction.

My mom left the other church and is now at a different church and wanted to get the girls for Vacation Bible School. She was teaching. She comes to get them at first. And then she starts making excuses on why she can't pick them up. The last day of VBS was supposed to be a party or something. I wasn't bringing them because I didn't ask her to come get them. The children were sad and I was pissed. That was just the beginning of disappointments that my girls were about to experience from my mom. Because throughout the year it happened frequently. My son is close to turning a year old now. Twisted decides that she's going to move in to her apartment. And making her sister leave. I was finally having my own place. Just me and my children. I could not have been happier. Finally, in my own place.

Season 13

Am I losing My Mind?

Moving into my place was like a dream come true. I had my job at the mail sorting company

at night. I loved it. Then I lost it. Twisted was working out there with me and the people didn't like her that much and they let her go. Well they thought I was having a problem with their decision and they let me go. I've had jobs and I've lost jobs. Yes, this book is about the battle that goes on for a person's soul. But the battle is not just Angels and demons fighting for you, but there is also a fight that goes on in your flesh about doing the right thing. I make sure to mention the jobs and the fact that I lost the jobs to show that I was getting punished for the life style that I chose to keep entertaining. Because I was still entertaining this spirit of Lesbianism knowing that it was wrong. Consequences do come for every choice. Going forward. So, I lost that job. Twisted started doing things that made me feel like she was doing something behind my back. I just kept getting this sick feeling in the pit of my stomach. There was a female that she had been talking to as a friend on the phone, that she met through her sister. Sick. I knew about the girl because I had met her to. And I knew that Twisted was conversing with her. I didn't think anything about it. Twisted and Sick had a brother that had recently come home from prison. They were so excited to have him home. I was excited for them. They

introduce him to me. I spoke a brief hello and immediately left. The brother came over to his sister's house quite a bit. We would drive him around looking for a job. He became very fond of my son. He suggested watching him whenever I needed to go anywhere. I was cool with it. Twisted started volunteering me to take her brother places. A lot. And she wouldn't go with us. I felt uncomfortable about because I knew how Sick and Twisted were. I was never disappointed. One evening, not late, Brother comes over to my house. We sit and talk. We had a very good and refreshing conversation. I was liking him a bit. We talked for hours. Until morning. Neither one of us were sleepy. The next morning Twisted shows up. I wasn't feeling guilty about anything because nothing happened. A week later I had gotten another job at Braums' and was working during the day. I come home to Twisted on the phone with this same girl. The conversation turns to me and her brother. Now I'm being accused of sleeping with her brother. I laughed at first because I knew it wasn't true. I tell her to call her brother and ask him herself. Men don't lie about sex. Not genuine men like her brother anyway. She never called him. But continued to be mad at me. I get my children and go home. Never wanting to come back at all. Twisted started an overnight job. She would come home and take a nap. Her kids stayed at my house so she could rest.

I was to call her at a certain time so she could get up and get ready for work. When I would call, she would be on the phone with this girl. She hadn't taken a nap or gotten any rest because she had been on the phone all morning and afternoon with the same person. Now something is starting to feel different. So, I wasn't going to her apartment much. I didn't need to, I had my own place. So, I just stayed at home. I continued doing what I would usually do.

At night I started getting the urge to pray and read my Bible in to the wee hours of the morning. I would fall asleep on my bedroom floor reading and praying. God was coming to me in dreams and talking to me about leaving this spirit alone. But I couldn't shake the feeling that Twisted was doing something to me.

The feeling was getting so strong that I no longer wanted to be in the same room with her. I couldn't sleep at night if she was over my house. I would jump out of the bed and go sleep in my living room. She started coming in earlier and earlier from work. Claiming that she was just so tired. I stopped letting her children stay at my house. I made her take her children home immediately after she came to get them. No matter what time it was. One night a police officer came to my door really late claiming that someone called and complained about noise coming from my apartment. I told the officer that I was asleep and so where the children. It wasn't my apartment. That was strange to me. And it happened a couple more times. The hunger and thirst for righteousness was getting stronger. I was making sure that I was reading my Bible and not missing church. I would get in my bed at night and look up at the ceiling and I would feel this heat moving through my body. I was just praying in tongues. I talked to Twisted mom about when do you know when you hear God talking to you? She told me to just be still and listen. That was something I wasn't used to doing. Mentally. But I was determined to hear Him, so I did it. And I just sat there. And He started talking.

He had been talking to me just not the way I thought He would. He came to me in the form of a brick wall once in a dream and there was a mouth and He was speaking to me. He said my name. He let me know that I was on the verge of slipping back in, but to keep

doing what I was doing. Slipping back in? Yes. During this time dealing with Twisted, she asks me if I was mad at her. I ask her why would she ask such a question. Was she doing something for me to be mad? She says no. I say ok. Shortly after that I get a phone call from the girl, she was letting me know that they were hiring at her job and she knew the person in HR. I wasn't going to go over there. But I did. I couldn't shake this feeling. So one morning after Twisted comes in from work. We're talking and I give her this warning about this girl. I had a dream the night before. The conversation turns into me being accused of just being jealous. That wasn't the case at all. Before I knew it we're now having a big argument about the brother and somethings that were talked about behind my back. Attacks on my personality. Attacks about the way I did things. People's opinions of me. The person that nobody liked. Then a battle started raging in my head. I can't exactly tell you when it started, but I know that I was having a hard time picking out my own thoughts. It felt like a sudden bum rush of everyone's opinions of Meekeeyah. From things that were spoken from my mom, my sister, my step-dad and his family, him, these twin girls. Their mom. My head hurt so much. And all of the time. I decided to go to college and I had gotten another job. I was working at Motorola. I liked that job. It was another escape from my thoughts and the people. It gave my mind something else to think about. By this time Twisted decides to pursue a relationship with this other girl. I tried not to act like I was hurt. But I was. I got so drunk one night. My children were sleep and I walk around to her apartment. Her door was wide open. I walk in and she's laying on her couch sleep. I walk over to her and touch her face. My mind was tripping. I felt like I was dreaming. What was I doing here? What was I going to say to her? I was crying and apologized for just walking in her house. And I stumbled back to my own place. I cried myself to sleep. Glad that my children never woke up to see me gone.

I had never been so drunk before. Thoughts of suicide were presenting themselves. I was comfortable with them. The next morning I get up and take my children to see my step-dad. I walk in and I'm just crying. My step-dad asked me what happened. I couldn't explain. Nobody likes me sounded childish. But it was the truth. I don't know who I am or who I'm supposed to be. My prayers were for God to do whatever He needed to do with me to get me to the point of using me and blessing me. I wasn't sure if my prayers were heard. I was tired of the chaos in my head. I was tired of this female. I was tired of me. Only because it looked like what everybody was saying was true. It looked like it.

The first night at the job there was a lady that was dressed in jeans, a hoody, and tennis shoes.

We spoke and that was it. The next night I was looking for her, but I didn't see her. She was standing right next to me, but she looked very different. Like a completely different person. I asked her was she there the previous night? She said yes, but I wasn't wearing any make-up, and she described what she was wearing. My mouth was hanging open. She was cool people and we clicked immediately. We worked together on the same line. We had each other's phone number and we would talk and laugh on the phone. There was this guy that wanted to talk to me and we ended up hooking up. I needed another escape. By now I'm no longer trying to even communicate with Twisted.

She was playing mind games and I was about ready to fight. One day she wants me, the next day she doesn't. So, I just stayed away from her. My new friend needed to move out of her apartment, but she didn't have a place to live. I let her come stay with me. I was happy for the distraction. Twisted kept calling me. New friend said I was giving her too much attention by even asking her what she wanted when I answered the phone. I ended up leaving Motorola.

I was having a hard time with my car and getting there every night. I was without a job. I wasn't worried about it. The new friend didn't stay with me long. One day Me and my kids went to see New Friend at her parent's house. Her parents were out of town.

We sat and talked. She started talking to me about God and purpose and a lot of stuff that had my heart beating extremely fast. The air in the room felt unreal. She was starting to look unreal. This person was put in my life to help shift me in to what I had been praying for. We were sitting out back by the pool and I thought something was going to come up out of it. She was just telling me what God was telling her to tell me. I needed to deal with the demonic activity in my head. I haven't been able to look myself in the mirror. My eyes were a different color. She was telling me all of this. She gave me instructions. I had to get some paper and pen and write down every thought that was in my head. Then I had to stand in front of the mirror and read out loud everything I had written down. I was like ok I'll do it when I get home. I couldn't leave until I had done it. I couldn't go back home the same way. So, I went up to one of the bedrooms and did what she said. Every thought I had I wrote it down. And then I said it all out loud in front of the mirror. My face was demonic. I was almost scared to keep going, but I did. When I was finished, I cried myself to sleep. The next morning when my friend saw me, she said I looked different and my eyes were back to normal. That was a serious battle going on in my head. I felt like I was losing my mind at times. I would lay in my bed at night just holding my head. I wanted to scream but I didn't want to scare my children.

Now that things were looking clearer behind my eyes, there was another battle brewing. One afternoon before the girls got home from school there was a knock at the door. It was a CPS Investigator. She wants to talk to me about a call that was made from the school about my oldest daughter. She let me know that she had been to the school and spoken to my daughter and staff. The allegations were of me spanking my daughter and left bruises.

I was barely even getting after my kids because of the trauma that was going on in my head. So, I know my daughter was lying on me. She more than likely didn't get her way about something. She acted like that. I had been warning the girls about going to the school lying on me. I told my oldest daughter that she's going to end up going to some else's home and when she's ready to come home she won't be able to. She just looked at me. So, the investigator talks to me about a Family Service Plan that included me not using Physical Discipline on my children for 30 days. I was cooperative with that. She also asked me about my plans concerning getting another job. She mentioned that they could help with daycare for the Summer, so I could have time to job search. The kids were almost out of school for the summer. And also, I was going to have a case worker do home visits to see how things were going. I was being cooperative. Twisted was calling me to take her somewhere. I couldn't leave right then, I was in the middle of something. I didn't tell her what that something was. It wasn't her business. So, the visit was over and right on time because the girls were almost out of school and my son was about to wake up from his nap. The next week the case worker came and did her first home visit. Everything was good. She complimented me on how clean I kept my house. I showed her the rooms where the kids slept.

We sat and talked a little bit about her job and some people she knew she needed to take their kids. Addicts. She gave me information to the daycare that the kids were going to start going to and that CPS was taking care of the payments. I was really happy about that because I had no money. The visit was over, and she let me know when she was coming back. The kids started daycare and my oldest daughter, her behavior was improving by not getting spankings but the younger daughter, she was getting buck wild. The morning that the case worker was to come back, my youngest daughter's behavior had reached its limits. She wet her sister's bed and tore up the diaper that her brother was wearing. Cotton all over the floor. My oldest daughter came to get me. I told her to run her sister some bath water, so she could get cleaned up before I took them to daycare. My daughter started screaming at the top of her lungs. I tried to calm her down I just wanted to talk to her. Find out why she did this. She wouldn't stop screaming. I couldn't hear myself think she was so loud. I gave her a bath, she was still screaming. She told me she was going to kill me. I wasn't afraid of her. I tried to get her calm. I just wanted to talk. I didn't want to spank her. But I couldn't get her quiet. I told her if she didn't stop screaming then she was going to get a spanking. I wasn't going to spank her, I just wanted her quiet. But then she started trying to fight me and I was trying to grab her. She fell backwards into the door knob. Then she was trying to get under my bed. She was having a hard time because the rails were low to the floor. She got up and hit me in the face and took off running out of my room. She started trying to fight my other daughter and I was trying to keep the baby out of the way. By the time I finally had gotten a hold to her I popped her with my belt three or four times and was done.

The case worker showed up, I let her in. I told her what happened and let her know that she had bruises and where they came from. She looked at her and told me she had to call it in. I was just being honest. I felt that by me being honest she would see that I was not intentionally trying to hurt my daughter. The case worker left, and I took the kids to daycare. After I dropped them off, I went to my cousin's house. My aunt was telling me not to run. I didn't know what she was talking about. Long story short I couldn't bring my kids back home that night. They stayed with the older sister cousin. It was supposed to be temporary. But it ended up a long time before
I got them back. I ended up giving up my housing and moving back in with my cousin to be close to my kids. This temporary process was wearing me out. The case worker was not conducting the case properly and was bribing and running off of every word my oldest daughter said. The case wasn't even about her. I ended up going to jail after moving out of my apartment. My son turned 2 years old while I was in jail. I missed my kids and I missed being in my own place. Catching a new case violated my Federal Probation so now I had to deal with

them. I ended up getting 7 years of probation for the Injury to a child case. But as soon as I came home and tried to get things back together, I had to go to jail again on the Federal charge. I was in jail for a few days. I finally came home, and I was lost. February 3rd, I went to my revocation hearing for the Federal Case. The judge sentenced me to 1 year and a day in the Federal prison. He gave me exactly a month to get things in order and turn myself in. March 3rd I was going to prison.

Season 14
You've Had It In You The Whole Time

Going to the Federal prison wasn't as bad as a person could think. I started off doing what people usually do. I worked out and watched what I ate. But that was not the things that started the forever change of my life. The day I met who ended up becoming my spiritual mother is what started the change. She asked me if I was filled with the Holy Spirit and I was honestly not sure. She said well let's meet in the chapel tomorrow and pray about it. I said ok. That whole night I heard voices in the air that it was gone, and I wasn't getting it back. Then fear started to settle in that I was going to make a fool of myself and fake speaking in tongues for this lady. I wasn't a faker, so I immediately blocked out that thought. I hoped that she was able to see truth. The next day we met up. We started out reading Acts chapter 1 where it was talking about the disciples meeting in the upper room waiting for the appearance of the Holy Spirit that the Lord Jesus told them was coming.

It came in like a mighty rush of wind. Then we prayed and almost immediately I began speaking in tongues. I was amazed. I honestly thought it was gone. I just kept speaking and speaking. I cried everything out while I was speaking. I was telling God about everything. I didn't stop until everything was out. The lady encouraged me to keep going. And that He was listening. I had never felt so free before. I felt like a load had been lifted off my chest and my heart. Me, the lady and another lady spent a lot of time together. At least as much as I could because I had a job and they didn't. I started coming to the chapel at lunch time, so I could get some prayer in. One day I walked in and the Lady was singing He Touched Me. I started singing with her. We got to the part that says, "Something happened and now I know, He touched me and made me whole". I felt a hand around my heart. It was squeezing the life out of it. No, He was squeezing life back into it. I was glowing. I was so amazed that I was feeling this inside my chest. My body got hot. I started shouting "He's touching me"!!! "Right now,

He's touching me"!! I wanted to keep that feeling forever. All that I thought was dead inside of me became alive again. I'm reminded about in the word of God where God asks Ezekiel if the dry bones can live. He prophesied to them that He, God would breathe life in to them and they shall live. (Ezekiel 37:1-5) He indeed breathed life in to my dry spirit and I was alive. I would sit and talk with the Lady about having a feeling that somethings had happened already. I had a feeling like I just couldn't explain it. She said You've had it in you the whole time. From the first time that you activated the Holy spirit inside you, you've had it. And once again you had to activate it. But this time you won't have to keep activating it because you are going to keep Him active in your life. But He's been there.

And those times that you found yourself hungering and thirsting for the Word, that was Him. You were starving Him when you weren't in the Bible. But He's been there, helping you get through every situation of your life. He was there. The same goes to You, Mr. or Ms.

Reading this Book. He's been with you and He's still there right now. I had a dream that I was in a motel room with a guy and he had gone into the restroom and I ran out the door. I felt strong in that area. I felt confident that I didn't need the substance any more to cope. I had found my high in the power of God. There was something still missing. I just didn't know what it was yet. There were some attacks from the enemy right before I went home but I just opened my mouth to cry out to God. I finished my pit stop at the Federal Prison. The Lady and I stayed in touch. But now I was ready to go home. I had lost weight and built up. My spirit, my self-esteem, and my body. I was a little buffed. Solid. Nothing missing, nothing broken. Not anymore. I was ready to go home and defend my life. God breathed into those dry bones and they became an army. Read it.

Season 15

New Season New Things?

New – Not existing before; made, introduced, or discovered recently or now for the first time.

Season – A time characterized by a particular circumstance or feature.

Isaiah 43:18-19 Remember ye not the former things, neither consider the things of old. Behold, I will do a new thing; now it shall spring forth; shall ye not know it? I will even make a way in the wilderness, and rivers in the desert.

Coming home from the Federal Prison started me on a new journey. God's power was much more evident in my life. Or should I say I was now able to see His power working in my life. I acknowledged it. I came home and made a very common mistake. I met someone, and we were talking about relationships and had sex. Not all in one day mind you. And I could have sworn that we used protection. I had gotten a good job when I came home. The supervisor told me that she pulled someone out of her training class to put me in. Thank you Jesus.

Me and the guy didn't really see each other because he belonged to someone else. Remember I mentioned early in the Book that people can come together for the sole purpose of fulfilling God's purpose. Stay with me. So, I'm back at my cousin's house and I'm working. I had to buck up to the Evil twin. I told him since he was determined to disrespect me, I was going to cut him with everything I said and every time I looked at him. I wanted him to bleed. Internally. And I did exactly that. It felt good, but it was not the way that God would have liked. Stay with me on that also. I had to let people out of my unforgiveness prison. So that God could begin His work in dealing with them. The Holy Spirit showed me everyone I needed to forgive. My mom, my sister, Evil twin, and another man. I had to go to each of them and apologize for not properly representing what I believe. I asked each of them to forgive me. My children were still at my other cousin's house. Going forward. The same battles that were in the present when I left, were still the same battles when I came back. The difference is, that I am not the same person that I was when I left. I handled things better and stronger. Still dealing with the same stuff at home, I poured myself into my job. Meaning I took advantage of all the over time they let me get, just so I could be away from the house. During this time of being home from prison, I continued my daily routine of reading my Bible at night before going to bed. The Holy Spirit led me to Jeremiah 1:4-10 3 days in a row. I asked The Holy Spirit was He trying to tell me that I was a prophet? After that my prayer life increased and God began to use me.

Immediately putting me to work. I had to give a word to the guy I was seeing from the halfway house. God had begun to give me dreams. Dreams with meanings. Warning dreams. And then sometimes God would start talking to me while I was with people.

I was introduced to a church from a couple that used to drop me off after work. They asked me was it ok to stop by their church for prayer night before taking me home? I was cool with it. It was church. And I needed to be there.

The week prior before I started getting a ride home, I was on the bus always having a feeling of urgency to pray. And pray in tongues. So when we get to the church, and walk in, I'm having a déjà vu moment. Like I had been there before. But couldn't remember when. There was an individual standing up praying. There was another man walking around tapping people on the shoulder and they would go sit up front with other people an they would pray and pass the mic. And then the next person would pray. At the end, the man that was picking people came to speak to me. I asked him why he didn't pick me? I tripped myself out asking the question.

But

I was feeling confident in asking. He stated that he doesn't pick new people for the sake of not wanting to make them uncomfortable. I told him to make sure he picked me next time I come. It was settled in my spirit that I was coming back for prayer. And the next week I came back and was given the opportunity to pray. And pray I did. I shook myself with the way I was praying. I sounded like a lion roaring in the spirit. Oh wow, was that me? I was excited. And soon distracted. There was a man at the job that was comical and cool. We started communicating quite a bit. But then some days I would come to work and it seemed like he was trying to avoid me. I became aware very quickly by some people that he was married. It seemed like once that information came out, he was normal again.

I found myself enjoying his company while at work only to have the reality check that he was married. I had a car in the shop that I finally got back. So I felt good having my car back.

Everything was going good with just associating at work. The couple that took me to prayer kept inviting me to come visit their church. Are you guys having a guest speaker? No. Just inviting you to come visit. Well I had to decline because I was in leadership at the church I was going to.

But one Sunday, I decided to visit and see what the rave was about. I pull up on the parking lot and couldn't even get out of my car due to the heavy anointing that was hovering. Oh my God, you're doing it like this over here? I was awestruck. I eventually got myself into the building. Praise God. Again I was having the feeling that
I had been there before. I saw the couple that invited me. And the other man. The married man. The whole service was amazing. I was warned not to look the man of God directly in the face. Why not? Because he sees everything. Well I didn't have anything to hide. The wild thing was this. The anointing on Apostle was tangible. I say that because you knew when the Apostle had stepped onto the parking lot. The anointing on him came in the door before he did. You felt it and then everyone starts looking towards the door and applauding. I was

outdone. Where am I? And I don't ever want to leave. The word felt like I was finally eating. Good food. I wasn't getting this at my church. The man of God was preaching, and got to my row and I swear I heard him say that I needed to come back. I was immediately praying and asking God how to leave my other church. After church, people were so nice and welcoming. They let me know that there was an evening service. I was coming back. I came back that night and that's exactly what the man of God talked about. How to respectfully leave a ministry. Oh wow.

That Wednesday night, I went to my church earlier than usual to respectfully leave it. I told the pastor that I respected what God was dong here, but I believe He's moving me somewhere else.

I shook his hand and left. In enough time to get to the new church for prayer. Time went on and I was eventually a member of this new church. I met new people and made new friends. It was

amazing. Only again to be distracted. The communication with the married man at work increased.

I had bought a new cell phone, because I was tired of not being able to use the phone at home. I was giving my number out to some people, and he asked for it. What? I don't think your wife would be ok with you calling me. She'll be ok. I gave it to him hesitantly. Some time went by and then He started calling me on a Saturday morning, letting me know that he was sitting outside my house. He knew where I lived due to being the one dropping me off at home sometimes. He would just show up at my house on our days off, and call me. He would park outside. I thought that was crazy. He would tell me to get up and get dressed. And wait for me, and we would run errands together. I didn't think too much of it. It got me out of the house. I had fun hanging out with him. There was no sex involved or anything like that. One weekend he tells me that we won't be able to hang out any more. I was wondering why. Quickly forgetting he was married. Long story short we started seeing each other on a regular. Come to find out he was having marital problems. So just as much as he was an escape for me, I was an escape for him. Two hurting people. Looking for something. He became my best friend. He shouldn't have been, but he was. One night when he was dropping me off at home, the Holy Ghost had me tell him something. And then at other times, we would be parked somewhere and I would get a weird feeling in the pit of my stomach.

I would tell him that we needed to go. He wouldn't leave and all of a sudden a police officer would be walking up on us.

One Sunday morning service, it came so unexpectedly during Praise and Worship. I was worshipping God and heard Him very clearly and as soft as cotton, "You stopped trusting me". It broke me down hearing it. I had hurt the Lord's feelings.

It broke my heart. I had stop trusting God to start trusting this individual that belonged to someone else. I was hurting God. And giving the devil reason to put me on the spot. By now me and this married man are in a relationship. Every Sunday hearing the Word of God we're being convicted about the relationship, and breaking up after service. Just to turn around and be back together Monday. Crazy. Everybody in the family was talking about me and this man. I was getting angry at the hypocrisy of it. I asked God why these people were having the nerve to speak on my sin when they do the same thing. He told me because you're supposed to be one of mine. You're not supposed to be doing what they are doing. I understood then. Every week I was breaking up with this man. It was crazy. So, on the first night that we finally get sexual, I got in the tub later and rolled over onto my stomach and realized I was pregnant. Nope not the married man's baby. I was already pregnant before we ever did anything. The guy from the halfway house when I first got home. Speeding the story up a bit, at 32 weeks I'm having problems in this pregnancy. I stayed dehydrated. I couldn't eat enough ice or drink enough fluids. I would get to work and almost fall out. The doctors kept telling me that I was too early to check anything.

But I wasn't. They were going by the measurements of my baby in a sonogram instead of the blood work. My birthday comes, and the married man takes me out to eat and pays for me to stay in a motel room all by myself. I'm there a couple of days and I hadn't felt my baby move in 24 hours. I went to the hospital; my baby was about to smother himself. The cord was wrapped around his neck.

I had to have an emergency C-Section. My baby came out crying and so did I. I couldn't have been happier. My baby was exactly 4 lbs. A baby boy. My smallest baby. And he was a warrior. He reminded me of myself. I was my mom's smallest baby, but a warrior. My baby had to stay in the NICU for a while. He was born with every odd in the medical field against him. He was deaf, blind, one operating kidney, he couldn't sit up or move his limbs. But God kept giving me dreams that he was going to be completely healed. So, I held on. And a fight came with that. As soon as I decided that I was not going to receive another negative report about my baby's condition. The fight was truly on.

One evening I go to spend the night with my baby, so the nurses can educate me on how to take care of him. He had surgery to get a feeding button in his stomach, and a colostomy bag. The next morning a CPS case worker comes to my room to talk to me. Yes these people are in my life again and over lies and false accusations. The social worker at the hospital had called CPS and tried to imply that I was abandoning my baby for not being at the hospital to see him. I couldn't get there because my doctor needed me to take it easy. It was my first C-Section and I needed to make sure that I healed properly from the staples. I had a medical restriction from my doctor not to do too much moving around. Including no driving.

But I would call the hospital every day all day and talk to the nurses and doctors about him. He ended up going into foster care before he was finally able to leave the hospital. I never got to hold him for a full 24 hours. He had been hooked up to tubes from day one. I now have a new car. Why? Because the one I had was older and had problems. And again some more honesty being used against me in regards to being able to efficiently take care of my baby.

You have to be able to take him to his doctor appointments.

How can you do that if your current car breaks down? The Lord covered me in that. He blessed me to get a new car. When I was able to go visit my son at the hospital every day, I found out that CPS told the staff to start limiting my visits with my son so that the foster mom could come. I was livid.

They tried to take me to court. They asked the case worker that worked my first case to come. I don't know why. But I saw her walking through the door and she was mad. Face just ugly about being there. The CPS supervisor tried to pass me some papers with a lie that I needed to sign them to get the court papers. I'm looking at this paper and The Holy Ghost says, "Read them first." I truly love The Holy Ghost. I looked at the papers and they were trying to get me to sign my parental rights away. I was pissed. I will not just hand you people my baby! Then I was given an attorney and she was approached by the CPS attorney. She tells my attorney, " I don't know what your client has done to these people, but make sure she gets her baby back."

The judge ordered for CPS to assist me in getting my own place. Which they did not. I was going off on people every day because no one wanted to do their job. Everyone was just sitting around waiting for my baby to die. And now I have to go visit him at the CPS office. I was so disgusted. And I'm still fooling with this married man. I was disgusted with myself. God told me to leave the man alone because God had someone else for me. I'm pleading with God that I would be the better wife. Please let me have him. God said no. Just because I would have been the better wife doesn't make him for me. In the process of dealing with my baby situation, The married man's wife finds out about us. Yes. I don't know exactly how, but it didn't matter because I was wrong.

I had to go to her after church one Sunday and repent to her. She was trying to avoid me and I caught her by the arm. She wasn't trying to hear anything I had to say. But I was being obedient to what God had said for me to do. This happened 2 times. And then I left it to God. We eventually have unexpected run ins with her and she was wanting to get violent with him. I would tell him to get out of my car and take care of his business. He wouldn't do it.

I'm pissed because she looked like she didn't care whose car it was, she would have damaged it if she had something. Her and I eventually start having conversations. And she began to tell me about when God told her to pray for her marriage and didn't. I was appalled. Why not?! And here is the result of you not being obedient. God allows me, a person that truly cares about your husband to come into his life to show him what the right wife would look like. And I didn't care how she felt after what I said because it was the truth. Our disobedience to God opens doors for the enemy. I say that because, if I wasn't already looking for something that I never had and he wasn't looking for something that he wasn't getting at home…. There would not have been adultery. God begins to deal with me heavily about this man. I would be at work getting dealt with. The Holy Ghost warned me of exposing my nakedness if I didn't stop. But it was now becoming harder to do. I'm about to show you something. When we are told to leave something alone and we don't, God allows that desire, or lust or whatever the sin, to get a hold of you.

So, where you were once able to leave that thing alone, you now need help. That's what the Bible calls becoming a slave to sin.

I wasn't a slave to that lesbianism sin. It didn't take much for me to acknowledge the bad affects that that sin had on me. The effects were crucial to my survival. I was fighting in my sleep. I would have dreams of being felt on and wake up feeling on myself. The devil. I was determined to bust out of that prison. This time that wasn't the case. I had moved out from my cousin into a motel room with this man. Almost every night we're having sex. I'm not the only one with addict behavior. He was using me as an escape from dealing with his marriage and being without his children. He truly felt like he had gone to far to come back. But God had me let him know that all he had to do was repent. God had already forgiven him. But he never repented. And then he loses his job. I knew that he had lost it before he got back to the room. He would ask me to use my phone and go outside to call his wife. We start to have arguments. If he wanted her back, then he just needed to go home. My Spiritual mother and I talked almost every day. And I had not told her about this man. She knew there was a man, but not that he was married. One day looking through the job ads in the newspaper, I see a company having a hiring fair. I decided to find me another job because the one I had was going through some changes and was talking about paying back advanced payroll payments. Management got upset with me because I mention that I needed to pray about it before committing to it. So my hours start getting shorter and shorter by the week. They wanted me to quit. But evidently I wasn't leaving fast enough. I got fired the same week that this man and I go to the job fair and get hired. He also moved into an apartment. I moved in with him. At this point I had no other place to go. I wasn't going back to my cousin's. And I'm the one with the car.

We are now having more heated arguments and literally braking up and making up. It was exhausting. That's the thing about sin. The Bible says that Sin is only pleasurable for a season. This season was quickly running short.

One day after moving into the apartment, the Holy Spirit asks me why I never told my Spiritual mom about the man being married? Was I ashamed? No. Then why haven't you told her? So I called her and asked her to forgive me for not telling her. She let me know that the Holy Spirit had let her know that there was something that I wasn't telling her. We continued the conversation and we're talking about different areas of my life that went along with the calling on my life. One Sunday morning I wake up to pray. I'm praying out loud for God to do whatever He needed to do to fix this relationship. Whatever He needed to do. The married man stops me cold in the middle of my prayer. Like ice water. "Do you know what you're saying?" Yes I know exactly what I'm saying. One day I get a phone call from my spiritual mother. She says, "Your Father wants to talk to you". "And don't run", she says.

Where was I going to hide? I fall on my knees to begin in prayer, and God shuts my whole mouth. Like I couldn't say anything. God says to me, "Why do you keep acting like I've never said anything to you?"

He started giving me instructions. I had to stop sleeping in the bed with this man. I had to move out when I got my income tax. I had to leave the married man. A few days later, I'm on the phone with him, telling him that he knew that he wasn't the man for me and wasted my time. I'm just going off. I got back to the apartment and we start having sex. Everything was good again, right? Wrong. Another day while we were having sex, a voice so loud and clear right beside my head says, " You need to tell him". My eyes opened so fast. The voice repeated Himself. "You need to tell him". I'm looking at this man on top of me. I begin to cry. He looks at me crying and asks was he hurting me? In a sense, yes. I'm crying hard now. And he starts crying. "Babe, why are you crying"? He says. So I go ahead and tell him that I was moving out and when I did, I was leaving him to. He hugs me so tight and we both continue to cry. I moved, but I didn't stop messing with him. I was so upset with myself at my behavior. The Holy Ghost had to handle me rough about this man. Get out of the car. Do not look at him. Do not speak to him. Go up to your apartment. Go in and close the door. Do not answer his calls. Even through my sin, I was still able to respond to the True lover of my soul. I needed that type of help. Because my prayer was to help me. He was in my bed again. And again. Sickening right? God dealt with me so tough I had a dream that I was running down the street screaming like a crazy woman. And people were looking at me like I was crazy. Then my older son appeared and told me that I was forgetting about them. I wasn't. But I was. Then I hear a demonic utterance come from my own self.

Then a voice said, "How long are you going to work for the devil?" Whattt!!!!!! That dream was so frightening that I jumped up and grabbed hold of the man in my bed. A voice says "He can't save you". I jumped out of the bed so fast and into the living room and fell on my knees and cried out to God to help me. I couldn't do this alone. I was living out all the curses in Deuteronomy Chapter 28. Read it. I was tired. I was still on probation for the case about my daughter. And Federal Supervision. By now I had just buried the new son. He died at 6 ½ months. But his ministry was to teach me how to fight until the very end no matter what the odds were. He was a true warrior. He fought until literally his last breath. I was then thrown into a zone I was not familiar with. This wasn't a miscarriage. I carried him for 9 months, birthed him, saw him alive most of the days of his life. I had a lot going on. I literally told God that I was a child in need of adult supervision. But I couldn't break down. That was never an option. One day I get a phone call from my probation officer, the DA was talking about issuing a warrant for my arrest. For failure to pay fees. The DA wanted to revoke my probation and send me to prison. I had to report every week and be prepared to go to jail. It seemed like right after I put my son in the ground things just started happening fast. No that's not it. As soon as I cried out for help. God began to move on my behalf. I would lay in my bed looking up at the ceiling asking God Why did He even keep being bothered with me? Every time He looked the other way, I was in to something. Again I was a child in need of adult supervision.

Season 16
Someone has to Die

Death – The cause or occasion of loss of life

Life – The sequence of physical and mental experiences that make up the existence of an individual

Live – Existing in Fact or reality

John 10:10 – The thief cometh not, but for to steal, and to kill, and to destroy: I am come that they might have life and that they might have it more abundantly.

Psalm 118:17 – I shall not die, but live, and declare the works of the Lord

I buried my son in March. By June I was getting exactly that. All the adult supervision that I could stand. I was going to jail. The warrant had been issued. I was reporting at the Federal Supervision office when the warrant flashed. The police took me to the closest jail for a few day and then took me to the County jail downtown. I asked God why I was here. He let me know that it was because I was disobedient. I couldn't do anything except repent.

Now I'm in the County jail. I go to court and the judge sentences me to 10 years. She asked me why I got behind on my fees. What did I do with my income tax money. I told her that I gave a sacrifice for God to do something for me. The judge tells me that the only required portion that went into church was tithes. 10 %. I told her that since I wanted more from God, I gave more. I almost hit the ground when I heard 10 years. I held my head up all the way back to my cell. Then I broke. My kids weren't going to know me anymore. The people already want to take them from me. What am I going to do? I can't do 10 years. I heard The Holy Spirit say" You're not going to do the whole time". That right there turned the faucet off. I was breathing calmly again. My God Mother would be in my dreams talking to me about how I should be conducting myself while being incarcerated. Oh I forgot to tell you. I was pregnant again. By the married man. But then one morning when I was reading my Bible and praying, I read about God removing the curse. The man of God at the church I was going to had already said that any baby conceived in adultery will die. I knew he was talking about my baby. I couldn't feel any way about it. It was the Will Of God. So now I'm in this cell reading about the removal of this curse. By the end of that day I was on the toilet having a swift miscarriage. I felt just fine. God didn't want anything tying me to that man. I was grateful. My day came to pull chain, and I went to a State Jail Facility. For 90 days I was there fighting this lesbianism spirit that kept trying to latch on. But The Holy Spirit was too strong in me for anything to ever happen. Thank God. I was getting mail from the married man and my emotions would be a rollercoaster. How crazy I was in my mind, I had the nerve to ask a man that was already married to marry me. I needed some help for my mind. So

Battlefield of the Mind by Joyce Meyer was handed to me by a total stranger. She just walked up to me and said here. I was starting to feel alone, so I started a journal titled, Dear Jesus. I would talk about my feelings for that day and whatever else was on my mind. I would go to bed. Then whenever He spoke to me, I would go back to the journal and record what He answered. It made me feel better. Every 10 to 11 months I was coming up for parole. The first time, the answer was no. I understood right off the rip that I wasn't ready. 90 days was up, and it was time to move to the Prison unit. Whichever one that was. I had to be honest about the situation. Lord, I'm afraid. He came back saying "No weapon formed against you will ever prosper while you are here". I was ready to go then. Let's get this done. Moving to the biggest unit out of 5 was a bit overwhelming.

It was rainy and started to get cold. It was also on a Friday afternoon. We would have to wait for Monday morning to get all of our essentials. Blanket, and clean clothes. Monday came, and I could not have been so grateful for a blanket. It wasn't plush or anything that you would by at the store. No, it was very thin. But I was so grateful, I was crying. Books began to drop into my lap that helped me deal with whatever battle I was having internally. It was preparing me for a battle that was coming. December of 2007, I began to get sick. It sprung up out of nowhere. I began to get really big blisters in my mouth. They were so big on the inside that it made my cheeks big on the outside. I woke up one morning and my right leg was so swollen that I could barely stand on it. I had been to the dentist and had my teeth cleaned, and that helped the situation a bit. When going to the dentist, because it was on a different unit, we had to get undressed in front of an officer. To make sure that we weren't trying to bring anything to anyone. So, as I'm taking off my clothes and undergarments I notice blood running down the sides of my breast. And not just a spot. Flowing blood.

A band-aid wouldn't have been big enough to cover this. I had to put sanitary napkins in my bra to cover up the blood. My skin had become extremely thin. What was going on?

And every time I had to leave the unit, I had to strip out of my clothes. I was horrified at the thought. I always felt like everyone was looking at me. I wanted to hide. One time a friend of mine helped me calm down by telling me to just watch her and not look at no one else. I hear you Holy Ghost. We're so much more concerned about people looking at us and judging us, when all we need to do is keep our eyes on God. Be more concerned about what He says instead. People will hang you on a cross, and make sure you don't die just so you can never come down. But even Jesus said before coming off the cross "It is finished". The decision concerning you is already established in the heavens. It is finished. Thank you God. I saw the doctor about my leg and I was prescribed the strongest antibiotic they had. It cleared things up with my leg. I was on crutches for 2 weeks. But then I started breaking out all over my body with fluid blisters. I also had gotten a pass that medically excused me from wearing a bra for 90 days. I began to have pain. And a lot of it, in my body. The skin on my bottom lip had peeled off. It was hard to hold a cup to my mouth. Fluid was draining from my body like a faucet. I began to lose a lot of weight due to not being able to tolerate the texture of food in my mouth. I didn't know what was happening to me. Other inmates tried to diagnose me. I had AIDS, or LUPUS. Or I was just simply dying. I prayed and asked God to just be with me if I was dying. At that point, that would have given my body such relief from the pain that I was feeling. It hurt to comb my hair. Clothes felt heavy on me. The Holy Spirit then spoke to me "You will not die, but live and proclaim my works."

That settled everything down in my spirit. I finally get in to see the doctor and I ask him if he knew what this was. He replied, "No, but I'm going to try my best to figure it out. And If I can't figure it out, we'll talk about sending you to the hospital." The inmate hospital was in Galveston. I really didn't want to go because I had seen that people never come back to the same place after they go on a hospital trip. The doctor took labs and gave me 2 types of antibiotics, Benadryl, and steroid meds to take every day. The Holy Spirit had already told me that they weren't going to find anything in my blood, but they were going to treat it. I was taking the meds for about a month and everything cleared up. I was starting to feel better. The Medicine ran out and I started all over again with the break out. I was like, what is going on? I thought it was cured. The Holy Spirit said, I didn't tell you that it would be cured.

I said they would treat it. So, this was to be ongoing? Oh wow. So, I didn't have to work at all. They didn't know what they were dealing with. While I was on this medicine, God began to work somethings out of me. I say work things out of me because one day I had this deathly smell coming from my body that soap and water could not wash away. I know that if I smelled it, others did to. I couldn't do anything about it. I was talked about even more than usual. People treated me and other people that were sick, like it's our fault that we're sick and can do something about it. No, I couldn't do anything about it. I'm sorry that you are feeling inconvenienced. I prayed and asked God what this smell was. He told me that the smell was all the sin and destructive things that I had done to my body. He was purifying me. He couldn't present me to my husband with all of that. And just as quick as the smell came, it left. I was pure. I was grateful to God for wanting to do this for me.

He's holy so I have to be holy. The Bible says "Be ye Holy as I am Holy". As I was in between doctor appointments God was doing things in me as well. I was beginning to have a greater revelation of His Word. God reminded me about when I was convinced that I might have been dying that I was dying. The old man, Meekeeyah had to die. He reminded me of a prayer that I prayed years ago. God do whatever you have to do with me to get me to the point where you can begin to use me and bless me. He said, I'm doing that. But in order for the outcome to be as I intend for it to be, you have to die. I was blown away by that revelation. I'm reminded of what Paul says in Galatians 2: 20, I am crucified with

Christ: nevertheless, I live; yet not I, but Christ liveth in me: and the life which I now live in the flesh I live by the faith of the Son of God, who loved me and gave himself for me.

So, when Meekeeyah died, Jesus began to have full reign in this temple not made with hands. Praise God. I was also taking some transitional classes. Cognitive Intervention and then another class entitled, Changes. Inmates take these classes the closer they get to going home. So, I assumed that I must be getting ready to go home. Not yet Meekeeyah. Not yet. By February of 2008, the doctor decided to send me to Galveston to the Dermatologist. I had to inventory my things and got ready to go. I was nervous, but I was ready to find out what was wrong with me. So, I went, and they took pieces of skin that had a blister on it and did a biopsy. When I got back from the hospital, I ended up not going back to the unit I started on. I was now going to the second biggest unit. I started off in a dorm and then was moved to a two- man cell. While in the dorm there was a list put up for people to sign up to be baptized. As I was walking towards the paper, I began to hear this voice,

"You don't want to do that". Then I felt fear. Oh, I see. Something great is about to happen and you don't want it to. Well then let me run and put my name on this list. This is how I was talking to the Devil. Now I'm in this cell with this lady who was treating me like I had the plague. She was so mean and hateful. She talked about me and didn't want me to touch anything. I was hurting so bad having to climb up and down on this bunk. I went to see the nurse and a good friend of mine was standing in the hall. She asked me how I was doing. I started crying while I was talking. Before I could say anything else, she had went and got a couple of officers. She said, "This is my friend and she's really sick can you please help her?" I was nervous. I didn't know what was about to happen. They told me to come in to their office. They ran the laundry. So, I told them what was happening, and they gave me bigger clothes and new under garments. That was the start of it. Next thing, someone got on the phone with the doctor and he sent over a bottom bunk restriction.

That meant I didn't have to climb that bunk any more. Next thing, they found out that my cell mate didn't have a bottom bunk restriction and put her at the top. Well I had let them know that she was giving me a hard time in the cell, so they moved her completely out. And I got my meds refilled and from then on, they knew me in the building. I had favor everywhere. From all ranks. The day came for the baptism. I couldn't have been more scared and excited all at the same time. I was 30 years old. Just like Jesus. I couldn't wait. So, when it was my turn to sit in this ice-cold water, I began to feel something brewing in the Spirit. I didn't know what was about to happen next. I was dunked and came up and everything changed. A few days later I had to pack up and move to the second smallest unit.

I thought someone had registered me for a Culinary Arts course that was on this unit. That's the reason most people move there. But I was happy to go. I get there and meet a lady on the recreation yard. She invites me to come to church services with her on that Sunday. I was going any way, but I said ok. We then met up on the yard again after church and we talked about God and the Word. Other women that were there were having testimony service and because I was new, I just stayed quiet and took everything in. I loved the Spirit that was on this unit. It was peaceful. And childlike. It felt wonderful. I was glad to be there. I didn't want to ever leave this unit. I wanted to finish my time right here. I was dreaming. That next weekend the lady invited me to go to rec after church. When I got there, she says, "You ready woman of God?" I said, "Ready for what?" She says, "The Spirit told me if I bring the people, you would bring the Word". My eyes got wide. I shook my head and obeyed. We all gathered in a circle to pray. I led the prayer and felt a gush of wind blow over me. I asked the lady standing next to me if she felt that. She just smiled. The prayer was over and The Spirit started talking.

I'm just repeating everything I hear God saying. These women were so entuned. No one moved until the last word was spoken. That was about

30 minutes. I preached my first sermon that day. All Glory belongs to God. I was so humbled and honored that He deemed me responsible enough to talk to these His people. The word was about Change. Which was very fitting for the current situation we were all in. Praise God. The next week I was moving back to the second biggest unit. My vacation was over. The big work was about to happen.

I would sit in the Day Room and people would come up to me and start asking me questions about the Bible. Next thing you knew we had a whole table full of people talking about the Word. And I was teaching it to them, by the leading of The Holy Spirit. I'm so reminded of Jesus after He was baptized and immediately started His ministry. He was in ministry 3 years and went to the cross. That's where I had to stop. Lord all of this is looking like that. Am I going to the cross to? I could feel God looking at me like Girl you are silly. I was serious. But only He knew what would happen next. I mentioned in another season that something was missing. I remember going to church services hearing this word over and over and over. Relationship.

Have a relationship with God. Lord is this not what we have? You can be an employee and not have a relationship with the boss. But God wanted more than just for me to be an employee of his. He wanted me to be His daughter. That missing piece was Relationship. I knew God and everything, but I didn't have the Relationship. And that changes everything. Having the relationship with God gives you a better perception on how your behavior should be. And it gives you access to certain things that everyone else can't have access to. Jesus mentions in John chapter 15- That we abide in him and his words abide in us, we can ask for anything and we will get it. That's benefits of relationship. When I mentioned that I bucked up to the Evil twin but not in a way that pleased God, I had to come back and make things right. To clear me. So, I had to repent. And forgive. And by me doing that, releasing him from my unforgiveness prison, God didn't hesitate to deal with him. He ended up going to prison for his biggest sin. Child molestation. The victim told someone. But that couldn't have happened right away if I was still operating in unforgiveness. Release those people today, so that the Lord can promptly deal with those people accordingly.

He can do it whole lot better and more effective than you can. I experienced a lot of things with people and their spirits since beginning to work for God. I have experienced people who have gained so much with God and then lose it because the enemy made them afraid. They drew all the way back. And blamed me. I had to deal with this.

God took me to Exodus where the Children of Israel did the same thing to Moses. I read it and felt so much better. Because the result was that the unbelieving generation did not enter the promise. They died off. I began to be afraid for people. I had assignments to spiritually battle for people. People would come in to my spirit and I had to pray for them. By now I have received the full diagnosis of this illness. The doctor tells me it's an autoimmune disease called Pemphigus Vulgaris. What? Disease? I have to take medicine for the rest of my life. I was having a hard time at first. But God just be with me. And we rolled on. Each time I came up for parole they denied me. I now understood that even though the start of this journey was about me, it's now about other people. I was ok with that. Only the Will of God be done. I have now moved to the smallest unit. It was so small it had two dorms. I had been here once before, but I was on another vacation. I'm back now and I'm working. God was giving me sermons. And even greater revelation knowledge of His word.

He took the story of Job and emphasized on his medical condition. He showed me that God used his medical condition for several reasons. To remove the ungodly from Job's life. As well as the people who weren't really on his team. His wife for instance. She told him to curse God and just die. God removed some things by way of this medical condition to make room for the greater to come. After that he obviously got a new wife because he had more children and everything he lost, God gave him double back. God was helping me understand why I was stuck with this illness. He let me know that as soon as it has served its purpose, it will be gone just as quickly as it came. I was no longer complaining about being sick. And I never had to work again my whole stay in prison. The doctor gave me every working restriction in the system to keep me from working.

But I wasn't completely unemployed. I was working full time for God. Studying and more studying. Praying and more praying. Writing and more writing. Big writing. Not just sermons, conferences. That came with deadlines. So, I had to eat and sleep paying close attention to God, so I could be aware of His next move. One day I woke up with the urge to exercise. So, I exercised every day for about 2 weeks and then the urge was gone. Replaced by an urgency to pray. Night and day, I was praying. Shortly after the urgency died down an individual moved in to our dorm. She was different. I was immediately drawn to her. And she to me. I helped her move her things in to her cubicle with the feeling I was supposed to be doing this for her. She said she needed somethings and I ran to the officer to make sure they took care of what she needed. And I stayed on top of it until the job was done.

The conversation was sparked with a common interest. And it flowed from there. She told me I was to be her mentor. I had to pray about that. I couldn't just take her word. I was praying about everything. I started mentoring her, and then it became something more that I had to ask God who she was. The devil wanted me to think that it was that lesbian spirit again, but this was something else. Something greater. God revealed to me that her position with Him was extremely high and important. He gave Moses as an example. But higher. I'm like what position is higher than Moses? She wasn't Jesus Christ. No not at all. As God was slowly revealing who this person was, revelation knowledge of what happens before a person is born starts to surface. This young lady told me about her life. As she was talking, The Holy Spirit was revealing things to me. About her parents. About her lineage. It's getting really deep and intense. I had just finished writing a marriage conference and God wanted me to teach it to her and another lady. The conference was for 5 or 6 days. But on the second to last day, the Holy Spirit had me speak Prophetically to them.

As I began to speak, I began to feel the intensity of the battle regarding this young lady. I had never felt such intense battle for someone before. God, I need to know who she is. As a fellow warrior with the Angels I needed to know who I was fighting for. Sure, it should be enough to know that she's on our side, but I need some answers. Please. So, I had a hard time speaking prophetically to these ladies because of the battle. She's just looking at me trying to understand what I'm saying. After that day I kept feeling the urge to refer to the young lady as Your Highness. God revealed to me that she was a queen. Not just any queen. His Queen. He took me to Song of Solomon. Who is the Wisest king to ever live?

Then He took me to Genesis 1:26 And God said, Let Us make man in Our image after Our likeness…. Who was He talking to? God also showed me that everything on earth is a reflection to what is in Heaven. Male and Female. So that means what? That God had a wife. Thus, the creation of marriage. All this was out of my league. I wouldn't have ever come up with that all by myself. His wife? There is a Queen? Whoa. You reading this book probably think I'm crazy, but you better believe that God will establish in your Spirit every truth that is in this book. You don't have to believe me. Ask God yourself. How she got here and the reason for this big battle, I'll let you doubters and unbelievers ask The Holy One yourselves. One night as we were getting ready to go to bed, I felt a presence so evil, it could not be mistaken. That dog was here, and he was here for her. The spirit of slumber tried to come over me. But I had to stay awake and pray or he would have taken her by the morning. Oh no. Not on my watch. A great responsibility was given to me at that moment. I had to call a meeting with the Angels. The General had to talk battle. I sat straight up in my bed all night talking to the troops. I was already given my instructions. I was waiting on the green light.

Then the voice of God came so powerful and piercing. EXECUTE him.

I had never heard the King's voice so angry before. But I didn't waste no time. My heart was beating so fast. God let me know all of heaven was with me. I was already hearing a screeching cry in the spirit. I took the young lady into the bathroom with my oil and proceeded to follow the instructions that were given to me.

I had to look her in the eye so that menace could see me and see who was doing this to him. All I heard was screaming in the spirit. And then it was done. He was gone. One thing that we need to understand is that we have to be careful about the symbols that we tattoo on our bodies. This young lady had the symbol of a serpent wrapping itself around her body. The devil was trying to completely own her. But she had the name of her love on her shoulder. The Word of God says how important names are. Starting all the way from the garden of Eden. God told Adam to give everything a name. Modern day idols are symbols of something. Understand the significance. Going forward be careful about the things you have put on your body. They open doors in the spirit to give access of your temple to the enemy. This young lady was sitting on a Capital Murder charge that she didn't commit. I had the assignment of reading her transcript. While I read it, God was revealing truth. Some truth is not always on paper. As you can now see if you have gotten this far in the book. After all the intense stuff died down God had given me another writing assignment. It was a leadership conference. 7 days long. I was 4 days in to the conference and God gave me the deadline of having it completed by my release date. I wasn't sure what that meant because I didn't know when I was going home. Or where I was going. I didn't know if I was going to a halfway house in San Antonio, or The Queen's house in Houston. I was no longer concerned because I was so focused on this assignment. By the 6th day I had received an appointment pass to have exit lab work done. I could not believe what I am seeing. I'm really going home?

And sooner than I thought according to the lab tech. She was able to see my release date in the computer. Oh Wow. I finished the conference that night and tried to prepare myself for leaving this place after being here for so long. 6 ½ years on a 10-year sentence. I had finally made parole. That part of the journey was finished. The Queen and I made sure that we had addresses and was going to stay in touch. Other experiences happened within that time with her but those are not relevant to the point God wants to make to you in this book. That's like in the Book of John where he says at the end that Jesus had performed more miracles that were not recorded in that book. Everything has a purpose in its own time. And now on to Freedom.

The Testimony Behind This Book

My youngest daughter comes to me wondering about who her dad was. I told her it was one guy. Someone else had told her it wasn't. Some time went by and she asked me again. I told her the same guy. My daughter reaches out to him on Facebook to talk to him herself. His wife reaches out to me on Facebook and we call each other to talk about the situation. We agreed to a date and time for them to come over and we all talk. On this day that they come, they bring an over the counter DNA test. We took the test. Waiting some time for the results. The results came back negative. He was not my daughter's dad. My daughter was devastated. She wanted so badly to find out who her dad was. And I felt like a failure. He was the only person that was never tested. Of course he was her dad. There was no one else. So I thought. I wanted him to be her dad, with the hope that she would be better than me. I went to bed sad for my daughter and wanting to erase the past. I prayed for The Holy Spirit to bring back to my mind anything that I had forgotten. I went to sleep. I woke up hearing this name. No!!! Not him!!!! I started crying because of everything that I had experienced and was still experiencing with this family. But him? I wanted to kill myself because of all the things that this man had done to crush my spirit. I wanted to kill him. Calling him- Evil twin was polite. But then after discussing this new discovery with the wife who is now someone I call friend, I was reminded of how it happened. From an outside looking in perspective. And she encouraged me to write a book. And here it is.

In the process of writing this book, The Holy Spirit let me know that there are people who have gone through similar situations and don't know what it is and how to call it out. My prayer is that my daughter understands the truth.

Prayer

Father in the name of Jesus. I thank you for each individual that is reading this book. Or have yet to read this book. Holy Ghost I ask you to show them selves in what season relates to them. Help them understand that the darkness can be defeated with the light. Holy Ghost let them know that You love them and have always loved them no matter what they have done. Out of ignorance is how a lot of mistakes are made. By reading this book, help them to learn from their mistakes. Change is what you desire for us. A new strength to overcome is what you desire for us. Your Word declares that your people perish from lack of knowledge. But it also declares that he/she who lacks wisdom, let him/her ask of God who will give liberally and without reproach. Help them to understand this relationship that you desire for them to have with you as I do. Holy Spirit I earnestly ask that you draw your people to a point of deliverance and accompany that deliverance with knowledge on

how to stay free. Help them understand that the ball rolls based on the decision to roll it. The ball of change can roll by rolling it. The ball of deliverance can begin by rolling the ball. You O, Lord showed us in the beginning of this book that Good and Bad results happen based on a decision. A decision to live or die. Deuteronomy Chapter 30 encourages to choose life so that we and our descendants can live. I earnestly pray that it be some ones decision after reading this book. Open their eyes to see what they have never seen before. Shed light where the enemy tried to keep things in the dark. Help them understand that there is an enemy that does not want them to live at all.

Father in the name of Jesus, I earnestly ask you to heal all of the hurt and disappointment that was dealt to each reader. I earnestly ask that you restore unto them the joy of Your salvation where the enemy has stolen it. Reveal purpose now in Jesus name. Make things clear where it was foggy. Regulate the mind now in the name of Jesus. Regulate palpitated hearts now where the enemy wanted them to be anxious, or even encouraged heart attacks. Help them to find all they need in you. Love, joy, peace, strength, relationship.

God help break these addictive behaviors. You be the only substance that they need to high on. Better than a man, woman, drugs, sex, shopping, stealing, drinking, committing crimes. Help them to understand that incarceration doesn't have to be a death sentence or a revolving door.

Help them to understand that freedom can be obtained anywhere You are. Help them to sleep better knowing that the Truth has made them free. Free to be who you called them to be and not what the enemy has said. Help them to learn how to have the same mind as Christ. Strategically position to be under the Holy Ghost teaching teachers, that will take care in teaching them everything that you reveal needs to be taught. In Jesus name. Help your people to forgive and teach them how to walk in that forgiveness. Forgiveness of people and forgiveness of You. Cleanse them from all unrighteousness. Take out the stony hearts that grew as a result of wrongs that were said and done to them. Give them a heart of flesh so that they can be in position to receive from you more than anyone else. Father I earnestly pray that their feet are set to walk the ordered steps of the righteous on the path of righteousness for Your name sake. O God. Have your way in your people. Let the truths in this book be meditated on continually along with Your Word. You are The Way, The Truth, and

The Life. In the name of Jesus I earnestly pray this prayer. Amen. To God Be The Glory

Made in the USA
Columbia, SC
01 December 2022

72458722R00143